FACE YOUR FINANCES

FINANCIAL ADULTING 101: THE SIMPLE, REALISTIC APPROACH TO MANAGE YOUR MONEY, PAY OFF YOUR DEBT, AND DEMYSTIFY YOUR PERSONAL FINANCES

JESSICA ROHRER

ROHRER PUBLISHING

TABLE OF CONTENTS

Part II

FUTURE FINANCIAL CONDITION

FACE YOUR FINANCES TEMPLATES

As you read through *Face Your Finances* I have some financial statement templates set up for you to use.

SCAN ME

With these templates you'll be able to work right alongside the book and have a clear understanding of your financial picture in no time. Scan the QR code for free instant access.

INTRODUCTION

Did you know that Americans have $1.7 trillion in outstanding student loan debt as of July 2021? Yes, TRILLION!

That is $1,700,000,000,000.

To put this in perspective, if you stacked one billion $1 bills the stack would be 67.9 miles high or about the distance it takes to drive for one hour at 70 miles an hour. That's one billion but what about one trillion?

One trillion dollar bills stacked up would reach 67,866 miles into space. You would have to drive for almost 1,000 hours before you would reach the end. 1,000 hours! If you drove for 12 hours every day that would take 83 days or almost 3 whole months.

And that's just stacking them on top of each other. One trillion $1 bills, laid end to end, would stretch

96,906,656 miles or further than the distance from the earth to the sun.

So how big is a trillion? It's HUGE!

And that's just the student loan debt, as of September 2021, consumer debt is over $14.6 TRILLION! Hard to even fathom.

With about 330 million people in the U.S. at least we know that debt is shared between a lot of people. But more importantly, how are we going to get out of all that debt?

Every generation influences the economy, but Generation Y or millennials (ages 24 to 39) and Generation Z (ages 10 to 23) financial behavior will have a greater impact on the global economy than any of the generations that have preceded them. Mainly due to student loan debt growing 7 times faster than the economy without financial education for these groups keeping up.

Right now the average student loan debt for college graduates is nearly $30,000 and increasing every year.

So it's a good thing we are all taught everything we need to know about personal finance and debt in school, right?

Oh wait… actually less than half of U.S. states require students to take a course on personal finance, even though it has become more important than ever to understand how to save, spend, and manage our money.

And yet only 24% of millennials demonstrate basic financial literacy.[1] Our future depends on these upcoming generations to help resolve this debt and yet less than ¼ of millennials have even a basic understanding of their finances and the need to save and budget. That's a pretty sobering statistic when you really think about it.

Most millennials struggle with simple concepts involving debt and saving. And millennial women, in particular, save on average $123,000 LESS than men and are twice as likely to not have any retirement savings as their male counterparts.

Almost 30% of millennials have overdrawn their checking accounts and 50% don't believe they could come up with $2,000 if an unexpected emergency arose within the next month.

Even more staggering 40% of Americans have saved less than $300 in their bank account.

My big realization that this was CRUCIAL for everyone, especially for women, to know was when I had one of life's curve balls hit (divorce) and all of a sudden I was completely and utterly dependent on my personal savings.

Several years ago I had a great job working at a large well known bank in the private banking industry in Washington DC. My husband at the time (now EX-husband) was working for the U.S. Government. He had an awesome job opportunity come up based in Brussels, Belgium. We talked it over for days, weighed all the pros and cons, and eventually decided, this was it, we were moving to Brussels!

I quit my job and we moved to Europe. If you've ever moved to a new place before then you know just how stressful the whole moving process can be. Try moving to a new country! It was quite the emotional rollercoaster: scared, excited, overwhelmed, and curious all at the same time. But I love chocolate, waffles, and beer so how bad could it really be?

We arrived in Belgium and started settling into our new home. There was a lot to get used to, new languages (Belgians speak French, Dutch, and German as well as English), new friends, new job for him, new lifestyle for me, new transportation system, new house, new country, new culture, and new life. It was scary but also exciting.

We had been there for a few days when one night we got into an argument and my husband turned to me and said, "I want a divorce." I was completely blindsided. I felt like time slowed down, all the blood drained from my face, and my whole life shattered. "WHAT!?!" I think I was in shock and couldn't quite process what he was saying. He couldn't possibly have said what I thought he said. But he did. I remember waking up the next morning and just thinking, "Oh it was all just a nightmare," and then the horrible realization that the nightmare was real.

I had a million different thoughts and questions running through my mind about our relationship and our life together. I will spare you the details, but some of those thoughts were, "Oh my gosh, what am I going to do?"

"I quit my job back home. I don't have a job here in Belgium. I have no income of my own right now. What the hell am I going to do?"

"Should I go back to D.C.? Ask for my old job back? Move in with my parents? Oh dear lord."

Similar to most married couples, we had a joint bank account where we both deposited our paychecks and paid for our expenses. A few days after he announced he wanted a divorce, my ex texted me and said, "I took half of the money out of the joint bank account, the rest is yours." We hadn't talked about it or made that decision. He just did it. It was gone. And there wasn't really much I could do about it besides pay my lawyer more in legal fees and suffer through a nasty divorce battle.

Just like that *snap fingers* in a matter of seconds half the money in the joint account was gone and I had no income. Talk about an unexpected curveball, ahh!

So here's an honest question: would you be able to live off of your savings if you had an unexpected emergency hit?

Unfortunately for most, the answer is no.

It is a scary place to be mentally, when you don't have financial security, and at first I had this crippling fear hit me like a ton of bricks straight in the chest. I was terrified.

Besides all of the emotional pain from what was happening with the divorce I still had, "What am I going to do? What am I going to do? What am I going to do?" running through my head.

Thankfully, I had saved a certain percentage of the income I made from my previous jobs in a separate investment account that he didn't have access to. So once I was able to calm down and think clearly for a few days, I realized I would be able to live off of my investments while I got my life back in order.

When I look back on this terrible situation, I am filled with pride. While I was terrified at first, I was ultimately empowered by my financial position and could make my next decisions according to my values instead of being forced into something out of financial desperation.

I could do what I needed to do because my financial position gave me options.

But I know this is not the case for a lot of people out there and I don't want anyone to wind up in a position where they are financially desperate. That is why I decided I would do whatever I could to teach everything I know about personal finance and money to help as many people as possible.

After some well deserved "me time" enjoying Europe I came back to the US, and moved to Nashville, Tennessee for a fresh start. I decided to stick with what I know best, finance, and started working at a nonprofit that provides lending and financial education to small businesses. Day after day I'd go into work and look at these small businesses' financial statements and be shocked at how many business owners did not understand the basic principles of finance. They had great products or services but their businesses and personal finances were an absolute wreck!

At the core of it, I knew that business financial statements aren't all that different from our personal financial statements. So sometimes those same bad habits we unknowingly obtain with our personal finances run over into our small businesses too and can lead to disastrous heart-breaking stories of financial hardship for both individuals and businesses.

The trouble is personal finance isn't often taught in school so the only place for children to learn it while growing up is from their parents. I was extremely fortunate that my parents started me off on the right track with my financial education. They didn't give me money, what they gave me was even more valuable, which was their financial knowledge. And although some people are fortunate to receive a lot of money from their parents, it can sometimes be wasted without the actual knowledge of how to manage that money. But a lot of parents are just as lost as their children are when it comes to their finances. So we see the same bad habits with finances repeat over and over again in a vicious cycle from generation to generation.

It made me realize that although we learn a lot in school unless you seek it out (and take Quantitative Finance courses like me) no one ever really formally teaches us about our personal finances.

This is crazy to me! Don't you think financial classes should be required?

Dear school,
Thanks for teaching us that mitochondria is the powerhouse of the cell, but how do we stay out of crippling debt?!?
Sincerely, Jessica

After all, we use money every single day and ALL have

personal finances we need to manage! I mean think about it, do you or someone you know make or spend money? Okay great, this applies to you!

Why not teach the real life things we all need to know about our finances? What about learning practical financial strategies for our everyday lives? Am I saving enough? Am I spending too much? What accounts do I need to open? How should I be investing? How do I get out of debt? Which loan do I pay off first? How much should I put down for a house?

I know I am not alone. It really got me thinking about friends, family, and clients who I've helped in the past with their finances. My expat friends in Belgium, my D.C. friends from home, my Music City friends in Nashville, my high net worth clients from private banking, and my struggling small business owners.

- Friends who have been overwhelmed by the thought of even looking at their bank account. Thinking that maybe the problem would just go away.
- Relatives who were scared to see how much debt had piled up on their credit cards. Terrified to know how deep the hole was.
- College grads who are unsure how they will ever be able to pay off all of their student loans.
- Family who couldn't seem to stop overspending on things they don't need.

- Clients who were ashamed that their finances were such a mess and had no idea how to fix it.
- Parents who wanted to save up and buy a nice house for their children to grow up in but weren't sure where to start.
- Colleagues trying to figure out the best way to invest their money and what accounts to use.

I have countless stories of friends and clients that could use a crash course on their personal finances. So here it is - Financial Adulting 101.

Everything you need to know:

- To actually have more money in your bank account at the end of the month.
- To be able to trust yourself again with a credit card and with your money.
- To stop overspending and throwing money away on stuff you don't care about.
- To be financially secure and take care of your family for the future.
- To put you back in charge of your money and learn how to invest it so your money starts making you money.
- To save up for your dream house in the perfect neighborhood to raise your family.
- Even better, to actually be able to enjoy your

money and spend it guilt free knowing that it doesn't control your life.

It's time for you to feel the joy of achieving your financial dreams and start creating the right habits to grow your net worth.

Together we will:

- Break the paycheck to paycheck cycle and begin living within your means right away.
- Secure your financial future and prepare for those rainy days and curve balls.
- Stop overspending on all the wrong things and start spending in ways that really make you happy.
- Understand your financial picture and organize everything once and for all.
- Tackle your credit card debt and student loans head on and look forward to a debt free future.
- Discover your financial goals and figure out exactly what to do to achieve them.
- Put you in control of your money instead of your money controlling you so you can trust yourself with money again.
- Look at simple financial best practices to make it quick and easy every time you look at your finances.

Okay, let me formally introduce myself...my name is Jessica Rohrer and I graduated cum laude with a double major in Quantitative Finance and Financial Economics as well as a minor in Mathematics. I was 1 of only 3 girls who majored in Quantitative Finance in my graduating class and I would absolutely LOVE for there to be more women in Finance.

I took a lot...and I mean a lot...of finance courses so I know all the theory behind finance, money, investing, asset allocations, risk and return, interest rates, and the time value of money.

I have been working in various roles in the financial world for over 10+ years including corporate finance, specialized lending, portfolio management, and personal finance. I've also worked with a lot of both very wealthy and not so wealthy clients so I've seen first hand everything that they do differently. But most importantly I learned how to think about money and manage my own money to accomplish what I wanted.

I love money, numbers, and finance and I love helping people to truly feel empowered with their money and accomplish their financial dreams. What you're about to learn is what set me up for financial success and has given me so many options and opportunities.

I am now in my 30s, have a six-figure net worth, multiple real estate properties, started my own small businesses, and have hundreds of thousands of dollars at my disposal. I bought my first home when I was just 23 years old, traveled around Europe for a year and a half on my own savings, and quit my full time job at 33 to grow my own business.

I am so grateful for the financial knowledge I learned early in life and am thankful that my financial position gives me the ability to spend my time and money where I want!

It wasn't always that way and it did take some time and effort but that's really all you need to succeed: TIME & EFFORT.

Nothing fancy required: no special degree, or specific background, or lottery winnings, or windfall from a crazy uncle, or special business plan, or massive salary. Just put in the time, the effort, and apply the knowledge you learn and before you know it you will have the financial relief and security you've been striving for. Once you get started you might even be surprised that it actually takes less time and effort than you originally thought.

I want to start you off on the right foot with saving and investing and set you up for financial success for years to come so we can all be millionaires and create an even better world for future generations. I want you to feel confident and empowered with your financial decisions and know that everything you want to achieve with your finances is 100% possible!

But also real talk for a minute here. If we're being honest you've probably been ignoring your money in one way or another for a while now. I've heard it before, and I get it, you don't have time, or you'll just figure it out later, or you're not good with money, or your partner will handle it, right?

The trouble is "later" never really arrives and ignoring it or just letting someone else handle it isn't really helping. (Don't ever give this power away!)

Instead, if you spend just a fraction of the time on your finances that you currently spend on Instagram or TikTok or watching TV then I know you can truly change your life! I mean for goodness sake the average amount of time we spent on social media in 2020 was 2.5 hours a day and the average amount of time spent watching TV was over 3.5 hours per day. PER DAY. I'm not asking you to give up TikTok or watching *Ted Lasso*, I'm just asking for you to take a little bit of those 2-4 hours spent on social media and TV and work on your financial future instead.

But here's the thing, every day you wait just makes it worse and more of a mess to clean up. To truly be financially free you have to face your finances head on and do something about it.

If you are really serious about enjoying your money and your life guilt free, you need to stop ignoring your finances, learn everything you can about money, and start creating your incredible future now.

This is your chance to be brave and make a real difference in your life that will continue to pay dividends (literally and figuratively) for years to come!

Here is where you begin to lay the groundwork for the path to becoming rich. I promise you the truth. What it really takes. No sugarcoating. And I'm going to show you how to take back your financial power.

By the end of this book you will have financial knowledge that you can use for the rest of your life and pass on to your children. Together we'll cover exactly what you need to know to truly understand your financial picture.

I promise it is so simple once you understand the framework. It doesn't matter if you aren't good with numbers. You can still do this! If you think you won't be able to buy anything you want ever again. Don't worry, you will! No matter if you are scared to know how bad it really is. If you start right now, this will literally be the worst your finances will ever be and will only get better from here.

Even if you're worried it will be a huge complicated process. It's easier than you think, I'll break it down for you! No matter if you've tried before and failed. This time you don't have to do it alone, I'm here for you! Even if you're ashamed or embarrassed by your finances. It's okay, we can get through it, I promise I've seen worse and we can make it better!

Do you have a calculator? Do you have a phone or computer? Do you have a pen and paper?

Yes, okay great, then you can do this. The strategies I show you work and will work for you. It works for everyone. All it takes is time and effort.

A little bit of housekeeping before we continue. To keep this book as straightforward as possible, I've split it up into 2 sections. The first half is all about understanding your current financial picture. The second half is all about crafting your future financial picture. Both are important. It is crucial to know both where we are and where we are going to truly create lasting change with our finances.

Often in financial articles I've seen these two topics commingled but they really are two different skill sets. So I spilt them up into part 1 and part 2 so you can easily go back and reference whichever section you need a refresher on as often as you like. The first four chapters are in part 1 and the last four chapters are in part 2.

Every chapter in this book will not only show you what to do and provide you with the tools for success, but will also give you clear actionable steps, called my *Money Movers,* to help you improve your financial picture. Please don't skip the *Money Movers.* Those are your checklist to make sure you've done everything you need to from that chapter. Take notes and take action.

I also have several financial statements and plans for your reference throughout the book with templates that you can use. Make sure to download those ahead of time right HERE so you are all set and ready to go.

If you follow the guidance in this book you will truly change the way you see your money and life will only get better and better from here!

Are you willing to do what it takes? Okay great, let's get started!

PART I
PRESENT FINANCIAL CONDITION

"The first step towards getting somewhere is to decide you're not going to stay where you are." - J.P. Morgan

If I asked you in 30 seconds or less to give me a snapshot of your current financial picture, would you be able to? Do you know where you are with your cash flow, debt, and net worth? It's okay if you don't know right now, most people don't, but this is really important information to know now that you have decided that you are going to improve your finances. After all, how can you improve something if you don't even know where you are beginning? So, in the first half of the book we will put together our entire financial picture, so we know exactly where we are starting from.

FACE IT, YOU DON'T KNOW...WHAT YOU DON'T KNOW

"Stay on top of your finances, don't leave that up to others." - Leif Garrett

Did you know that just looking at your financial statements will increase the amount of money in your bank account?

Just this simple act will literally make those $$$ magically start increasing in your bank account right before your very eyes.

Okay, maybe it's not quite like that...but truly just bringing some awareness to your finances will automatically help you start to improve them. The more positive attention you give to your money the more it will increase.

Have you ever heard that old phrase, "What you don't know won't hurt you?"

This may be a noble sentiment when applied to spare

someone's feelings. However, when applied to your finances, 100% of what you don't know about your finances WILL hurt you!

In fact, most problems I know of are best met with knowledge rather than ignorance.

So, I beg you...please stop burying your head in the sand when it comes to your money. You are hurting yourself, your family, your friends, your pets, and even future generations by not facing your finances head on.

Take my friend Emma for instance. She was a smart girl, with a fantastic job in digital marketing which she really loved. She was really starting to make some good money too. I always love to see that! The problem was she was TERRIFIED to look at her bank statements at the end of each month. She was completely stressed out by her finances and somehow it seemed like no matter what she did she was always just barely breaking even at the end of the month and still living paycheck to paycheck. She had tried budgeting before and every time she tried it just didn't work. She knew she made quite a bit of money but she also knew she was spending quite a lot of it too. She figured, "Hey, I work hard for my money, I deserve to spend it and treat myself!"

And she is right...and wrong. All at the same time. She is 100% right that she works hard for her money and deserves to spend it BUT she also deserves to save it and invest it in herself too! If she isn't really looking at her finances and doesn't know what's going on with them, then she isn't really choosing at all, she is just reacting.

She isn't making a conscious choice to spend, or to save, or to invest, she is just falling into an unconscious habit.

There are millions of dollars worth of advertisements out there that we are bombarded with every single day. They are designed for one purpose and one purpose only - to convince YOU to give THEM your money.

Is that really what Emma wants to do with her money? Maybe...but also maybe not. It depends on her current financial picture, so what does her financial picture look like?

If she is financially sound and has allocated money for shopping in her *Saving & Spending Plan*, by all means, take a trip to Nordstrom, enjoy it, and have fun! The key is to make sure it is truly an informed and conscious choice that you are happy and comfortable making based on your financial situation. Not just a default, unconscious habit that may not be in your financial best interest and could jeopardize your ability to cover the water bill that month.

It is ALWAYS in a company's best interest for you to give them your money. However, it is NOT always in YOUR best interest to give them your money.

It is in your best interest to make a conscious choice about what to do with your money.

So, what do we need to know in order to start making choices in our own best interest?

That, my dear, would be your financial picture!

WHAT IS MY FINANCIAL PICTURE?

Your financial picture is really just a snapshot of your cash flow, your debt, and your wealth. I like to think of it as one of those little old polaroid pictures with a summary of your financial situation in one easy to read snapshot.

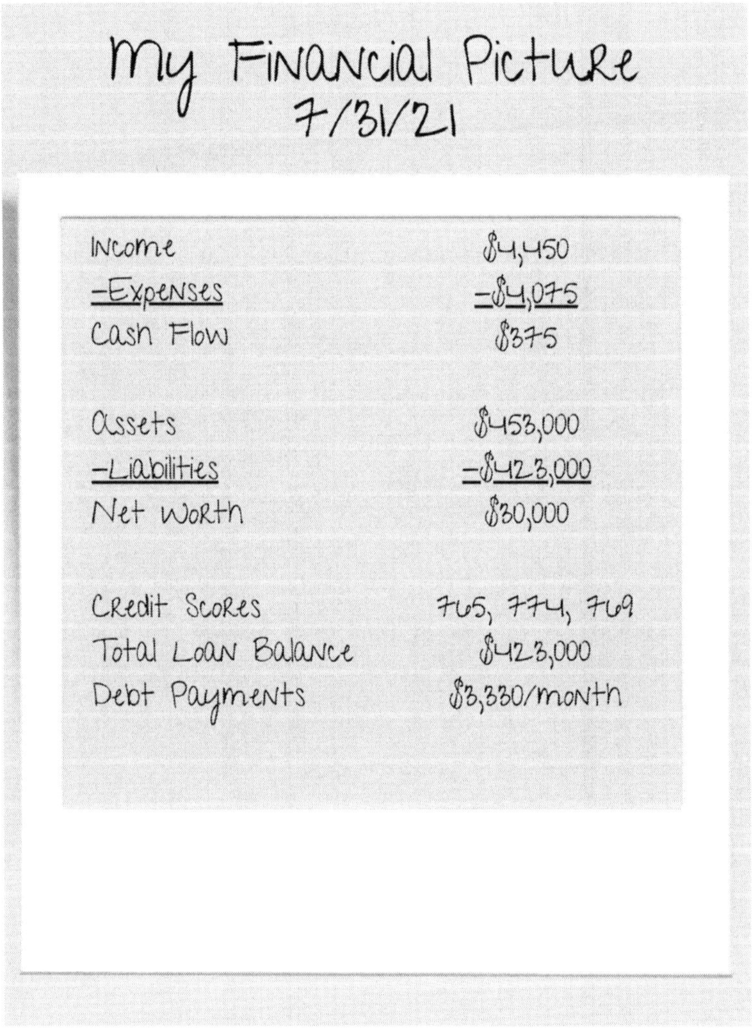

See that's not too complicated, right? I can hear you already, "Yeah, easy for you, but I have no idea what my numbers are, where to find them, or how to put them all nice and lined up like that! What's even the difference between assets and liabilities anyway?"

I'm glad you have questions and it's okay if you don't know how to fill this out yet. This is just the first step and we will figure out all of your numbers throughout this book. By the end of the book, you will not only know your financial picture, but you will also know how to keep track of it consistently, and, even more importantly, start to improve it!

If you look back at the illustration, you'll notice I have 3 sections in your financial picture and those 3 sections make up the 3 most important financial statements for you to know:

1. *Income & Expense Statement*
2. *Net Worth Statement*
3. *Debt Schedule*

I've added them to the financial picture in the next image so you can see which financial statements coincide with each section.

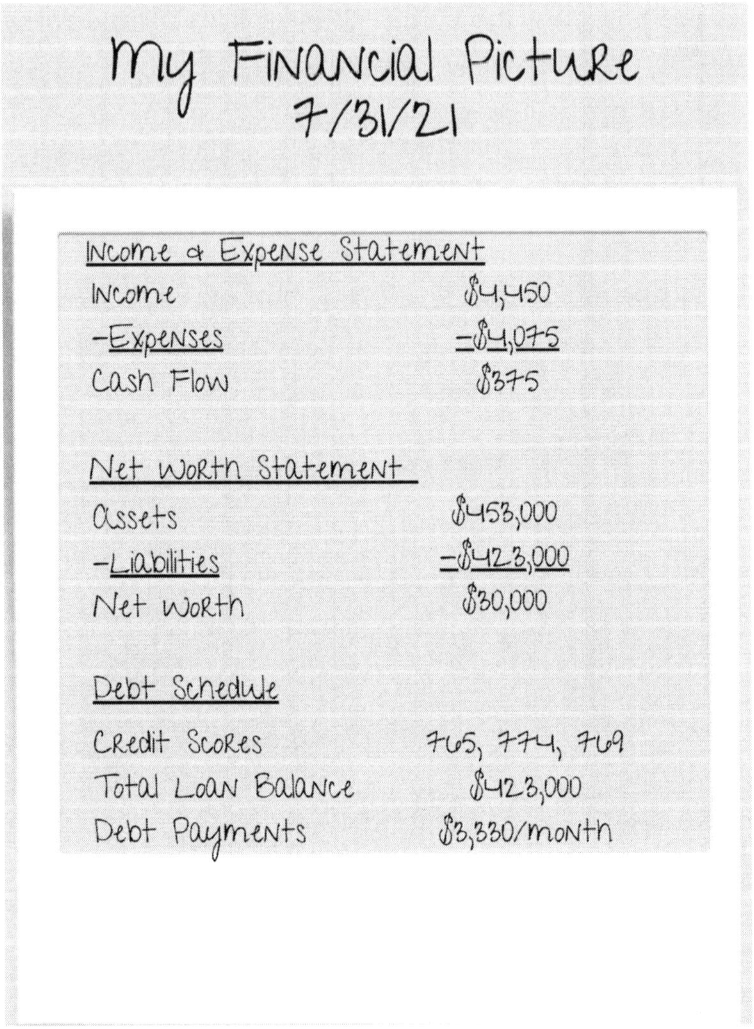

My Financial Picture
7/31/21

Income & Expense Statement

Income	$4,450
-Expenses	-$4,075
Cash Flow	$375

Net Worth Statement

Assets	$453,000
-Liabilities	-$423,000
Net Worth	$30,000

Debt Schedule

Credit Scores	765, 774, 769
Total Loan Balance	$423,000
Debt Payments	$3,330/month

Let's break this down even further and find out what each of these 3 sections are all about.

The first section references your *Income & Expense Statement,* which shows the health of your cash flow. This is your income minus your expenses which equals your cash flow. We will cover this statement in depth in chapter

2. I'm sure this is no surprise to you, but the goal is to have more cash coming in than cash going out.

Income & Expense Statement	
Income	$4,450
-Expenses	-$4,075
Cash Flow	$375

The second section refers to your *Net Worth Statement,* which shows how rich or poor you are. This is your assets minus your liabilities which equals your net worth. We will cover this statement in depth in chapter 4, and, to state the obvious, we want to have a positive net worth. The more, the better.

Net Worth Statement	
Assets	$453,000
-Liabilities	-$423,000
Net Worth	$30,000

Lastly, we have your *Debt Schedule,* which shows what you owe to others. This includes your current credit scores, which reflect your creditworthiness to lenders, your total loan balance, and the payments you owe for those loans. We will cover this statement in depth in chapter 3. Ideally, we want the debt you owe to others to be as low as possible. Although, not all debt is bad, but I am getting ahead of myself. More on good debt versus bad debt later in chapter 7.

Debt Schedule	
Credit Scores	765, 774, 769
Total Loan Balance	$423,000
Debt Payments	$3,330/month

HOW DO THESE STATEMENTS RELATE TO ONE ANOTHER?

You need to know all 3 of your financial statements to have a complete understanding of your financial picture. I'll provide a quick intro to each of these statements and look at how all 3 of your personal financial statements are related to one another.

On your *Income & Expense Statement* you have money coming in (income) and money going out (expenses). Your income minus your expenses equals your cash flow. At the end of the month you will either have either positive or negative cash flow.

- Positive cash flow = more money coming in than going out
- Negative cash flow = more money going out than coming in

When the amount of money coming in and going out is the exact same you are "breaking even."

On your *Net Worth Statement* you have assets (what you own) and liabilities (what you owe). Your assets minus your liabilities results in your net worth. Your net worth can be increased with positive cash flow or decreased with negative cash flow.

- Positive cash flow = increasing net worth
- Negative cash flow = decreasing net worth

On your *Debt Schedule* you have all the details of the loans that you owe to others. Your debt can be decreased with positive cash flow or increased with negative cash flow.

- Positive cash flow = decreasing debt
- Negative cash flow = increasing debt

Now, let's take a look at 2 scenarios with positive cash flow at the end of the month to see what happens on our financial statements. Let's say you have some extra cash still in your bank account at the end of the month, woohoo! Do you:

1. Put that money into a savings or investment account?
2. Pay down your student loan balance?

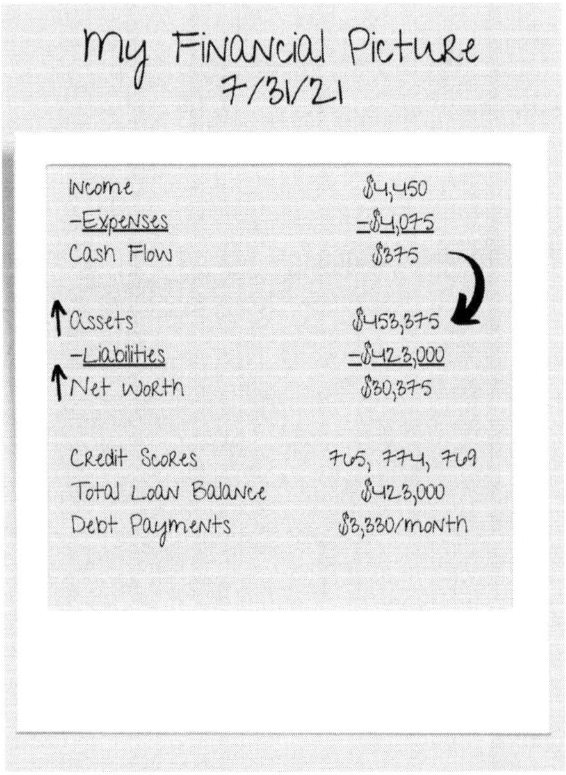

In scenario 1 with this first chart, if you put that money into an investment account for an emergency fund, then you are increasing your assets, which will increase the net worth on your *Net Worth Statement*. You'll see how both the assets and net worth increased by $375.

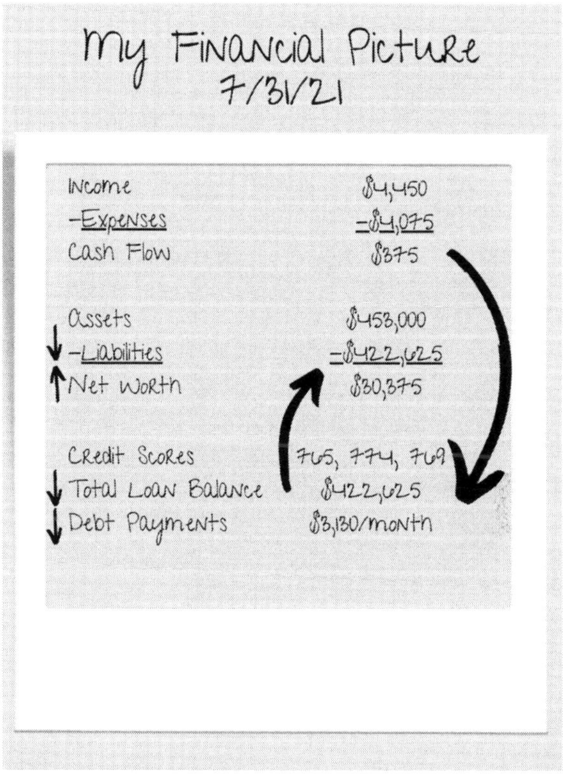

In scenario 2, if you are paying down your student loans, then we begin to involve the *Debt Schedule*. When you pay off the debt on your *Debt Schedule*, this decreases the total loan balance and loan payments on your *Debt Schedule*. This then decreases your liabilities, and increases the net worth on your *Net Worth Statement*. In the second chart, you'll notice that the liabilities decreased by $375 and the net worth increased by $375.

In both of these scenarios, you have positive cash flow at the end of the month, and you have increased your net worth. If you have positive cash flow every month you will see your net worth continue to increase. This is how we build wealth, by either increasing our assets and/or decreasing our liabilities. This is our big takeaway. Positive cash flow steadily increases our net worth, which is how we build wealth.

Next, let's take a look at 2 scenarios with negative cash flow at the end of the month. Think back to around the holidays when you bought Christmas presents for your friends and family. You knew Christmas was going to take place on December 25th and you knew you would probably spend more than your normal monthly income in December. Did you:

1. Save up all year in a Christmas fund to buy all your Christmas presents for when good old Saint Nick came to visit?
2. Buy all your presents the week before Christmas on a credit card?

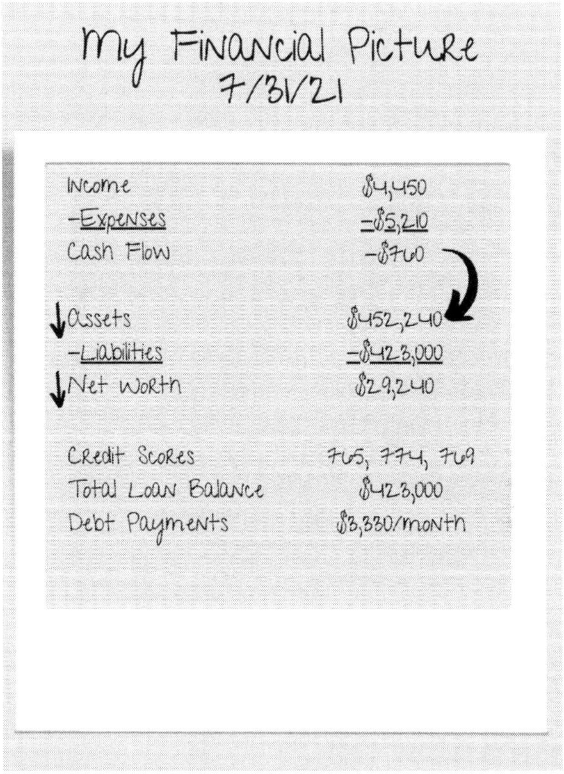

Let's start with the first scenario. If you created a Christmas fund you were putting money aside in a savings or investment account which is an asset. When you take that money out of your savings or investment account to buy lots of wonderful presents, you decrease your assets and the net worth on the *Net Worth Statement*. However, you spread joy to your friends and family which is a wonderful thing. And hey, you were able to cover your extra Christmas expenses for the month with your current assets and not go into additional debt, which is a good thing!

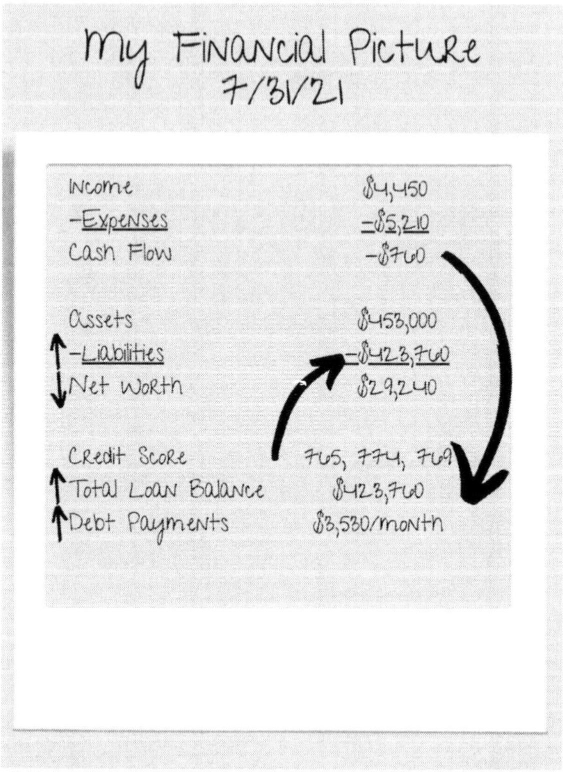

If, instead, you forgot to save up and so you bought all your presents on a credit card, which you intended to pay off next year, you were going into debt to cover your expenses. I see this scenario a lot with credit card debt. You basically just borrowed money from American Express (or another credit card) to buy your Christmas presents because you did not have enough cash flow or assets saved up to pay for those presents. This increased the debt on your *Debt Schedule*, increased your liabilities, and decreased your net worth on the *Net Worth Statement*.

Notice how in both cases there is negative cash flow of -$760 and this decreases your net worth by that amount.

At the end of the month, what happens on your *Income & Expense Statement* and on your *Debt Schedule* directly impacts what happens to your *Net Worth Statement* and whether you become richer or poorer.

Everything we do with our other financial statements is all in an effort to increase our net worth. So, in order to become very very rich there are just 2 things you need to remember from all of this:

1. Positive cash flow makes you RICH
2. Negative cash flow makes you POOR

I don't need you to remember every detail of how each of these statements are related, but I do want you to remember that all 3 are important and all 3 are related to one another, which is why you need to understand all of them.

HOW WILL THESE STATEMENTS HELP?

Okay you might still be wondering, "How will preparing and looking at these statements actually help me increase my net worth?"

Well your financial statements are just tools that show you the health of your finances. The same way it is important to take care of your body it is also important to take care of your money.

I want a healthy body so that I don't get sick and can live my life full of energy and happiness. I also want to take care of the health of my money so I don't get into overwhelming debt, can afford amazing vacations, and can buy my dog all the toys he could ever want.

Keeping updated financial statements allows me to track how my financial health improves or declines over time.

"If you can't measure it, you can't manage it." - Peter Drucker

If you take a minute to think about this quote, it should quickly become clear how very true it is. If you can't measure something, and understand the results, then how can you possibly improve the results?

For example, how would you lose weight without stepping on a scale every once in a while to measure your results. It would be difficult to track your progress and see whether you are really losing weight each day or not.

Makes sense, right? It is the same when it comes to your finances. Your financial statements are your tools for measuring your progress and provide invaluable information to help you change your financial picture and improve your life.

Knowing my financial picture allows me to know where I stand financially therefore I am better informed when I have to make a choice or decision related to money, such as, whether or not to buy a house.

My financial statements give me the information I need to make informed decisions and choices about my money and my life in my own best interest. It empowers me to make the right decisions for me and for my family, and I am all for anything that empowers me and improves my life!

WHAT ARE MY START AND FINISH LINE?

Now I know you picked up this book for a reason and are ready to change your financial future. Before we dive into the next chapter, let's just get very clear on where you currently stand and what you hope to achieve as you read the rest of this book.

We can do this with a simple 5 minute clarity mapping tool I first heard about from Dean Graziosi which consists of 4 parts:

1. Current Status
2. One Year Look Back
3. The Why
4. Capabilities Needed

You can use this template or set up your page to look something like this.

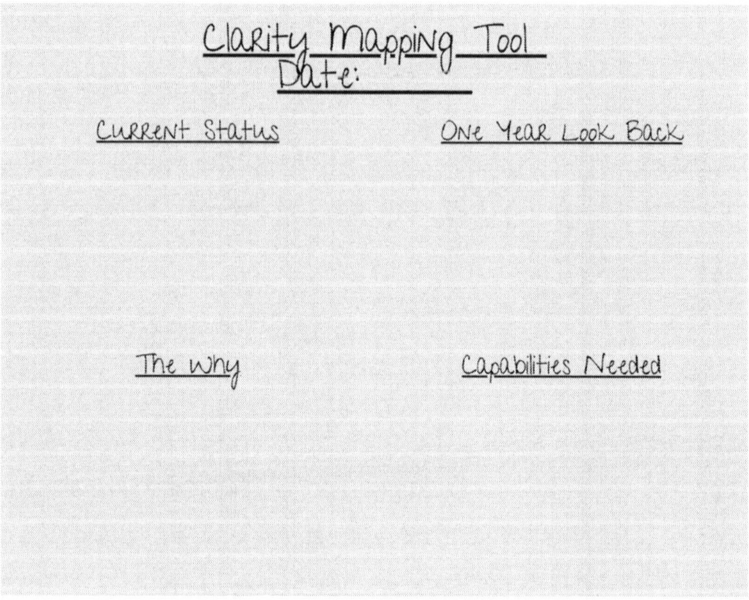
Clarity Mapping Tool
Date:
Current Status
One Year Look Back
The Why
Capabilities Needed

First, if you are honest with yourself, what is your current financial status?

What is going well with your finances and what is going wrong with your finances? What has ignoring your finances cost you both mentally and financially in the past? Have you tried to create a budget or figure out your finances, but it hasn't quite worked? What has this cost you emotionally? Stress, overwhelm, anxiety, sleep, anger? What about financially? What actual money has this cost you? What else has it cost you? Interest income, a new house, a vacation, gifts for your spouse or children? I encourage you to be as honest with yourself as possible.

Second, if you were to look back on your life one year from today, what would financial success look like for you?

What do you hope to have accomplished one year from now? You picked up this book because you want to improve something about your finances. If there was one thing you'd like to focus on and have accomplished by the end of the book what would it be? Would you like to understand your financial picture? Would you like to have a plan to pay off one of your loans? Would you like to have an emergency fund set up? What would the best financial year of your life look like? How would you feel? What would you have achieved? Whatever it may be, let's set that intention now and paint the picture of your new financial status one year from today.

Third, why are these goals important for you to achieve?

Why is it important for you to get your finances in order right now and not wait any longer? Is your credit score hurting your ability to buy a house? Has your debt piled up so much that it feels like it has gotten out of control? Are you tired of waking up in the middle of the night stressed about your bank account balance and whether or not you can cover this month's bills? Just take a few minutes and think about why it is really important to address your finances right now.

Lastly, what capabilities do you need to cultivate in yourself in order to achieve these goals?

In order to accomplish what you have outlined for your financial success, what are the skills or capabilities that you would need? What would that financially successful person look like? What abilities would they have? Would they need courage? Or consistent action? What about becoming a leader? Or arc there very specific skills you would need? What about confidence? Write down a few different skills you would need in order to achieve your goals.

Here is an example of the clarity mapping tool.

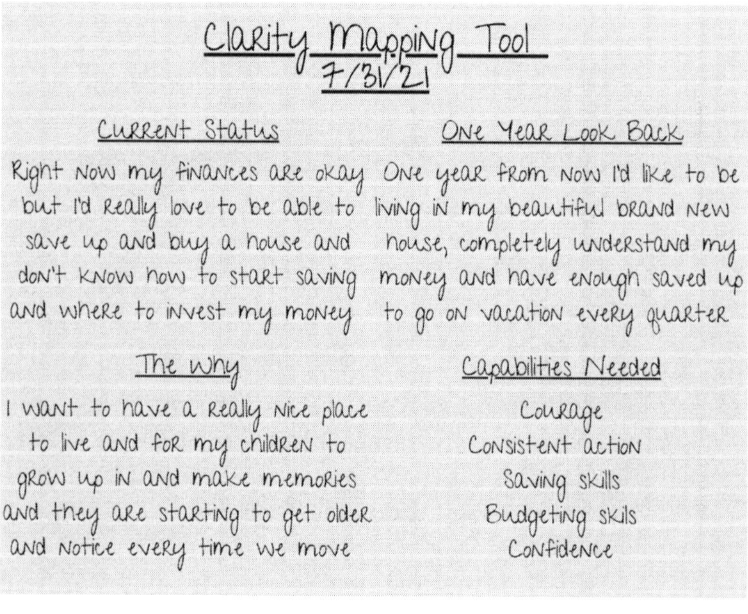

Clarity Mapping Tool
7/31/21

Current Status

Right now my finances are okay but I'd really love to be able to save up and buy a house and don't know how to start saving and where to invest my money

One Year Look Back

One year from now I'd like to be living in my beautiful brand new house, completely understand my money and have enough saved up to go on vacation every quarter

The why

I want to have a really nice place to live and for my children to grow up in and make memories and they are starting to get older and notice every time we move

Capabilities Needed

Courage
Consistent action
Saving skills
Budgeting skils
Confidence

Grab a pen and paper and take about 5 minutes to quickly go through and answer the questions from this exercise. I suggest grabbing a journal so you have everything written down in one place as you go through the book. I could explain all the reasons why physically writing this down is important, but we have more finance topics to cover, so I'll save that for another book. Please just trust me, it is important!

Understanding your answers to these questions will help keep you motivated throughout the book. Whenever you start to doubt yourself you can always look back and read through them and remind yourself why you are doing this!

MONEY MOVERS

Chapter 1 complete. You are doing great, keep it up! At the end of each chapter, I'll have a few action items for you to take called *Money Movers* that will help you move the needle with your money and implement what you've learned. Please don't skip them, these are what help you succeed.

- Find pen and paper. Or really any writing utensil and a journal, so you can keep everything together in one place. It doesn't have to be fancy, it can be your daughter's crayon and a $2 notebook from Target for all I care.
- Take 5 minutes to complete the clarity mapping tool: 1) Current Status 2) One Year Look Back 3) The Why 4) Capabilities Needed

INCOME & EXPENSE STATEMENT

"Making more money will not solve your problems if cash flow management is your problem." - Robert Kiyosaki

Time to dive into our very first financial statement…the *Income & Expense Statement*. We are starting here because CASH IS KING! Your cash flow affects everything else in your financial picture so it is the most important to understand first.

One thing I've noticed with profitable business owners is that they are very keenly aware of what is going on with their cash flow. On the flip side, when working with my struggling business owners, whenever there is a problem I almost always can point back to cash flow as the source of the problem.

> "Never take your eyes off the cash flow because it's the life blood of business." - Richard Branson

And it is not just important for business finances. The same goes for your personal finances as well. Everything in your other two financial statements (your *Net Worth Statement* and your *Debt Schedule*) stems from what is happening in your *Income and Expense Statement* and whether you have positive or negative cash flow.

Positive cash flow creates incredible wealth and riches. Negative cash flow creates debt and financial ruin.

And it DOES NOT MATTER how much you earn. Chris Hogan's new book, *Everyday Millionaires,* talked about a study of 10,000 millionaires. Of these millionaires 69% did it with an income of less than $100,000 a year. LESS than $100,000 a year! I know a lot of people who make less than $100,000 a year so I know it is possible for us all to become millionaires.

I also see a lot of examples of people just barely breaking even in their finances just like in Cory Faucett's article, "Why Many Doctors Live Paycheck to Paycheck."

> "Rather than becoming wealthy, many doctors today are HENRYs: High Earners, Not Rich Yet. Many doctors feel the need to spend all, or more than all, of their income. They worked hard to become

> doctors, and now they want to reap the benefits by spending their earnings. They are the "working rich." They only appear rich as long as they are working. If they were to stop working, they would be broke."
>
> "I recently wrote about a family that was earning $750,000 a year and had been doing so for some time. They had a net worth of near zero. How can one earn so much, yet have so little? It's because every dollar they earned was spent on their very nice lifestyle. Nothing was set aside for saving and investing. They needed all their earnings to "get by." This is laughable to those who "get by" on only $100,000 annually and still become millionaires." - Cory Faucett

---

It is mind boggling...and also very sad. These people are given an absolutely incredible opportunity to completely change their lives with the amount of money they have access to. But because they have failed to learn the simple concept of living within their means, they are wasting the opportunity that money provides.

Unfortunately, I have also seen cases of extreme negative cash flow over and over again in the tabloids. Larry King, George Foreman, Wayne Newton, Kim Basinger, Burt Reynolds, Elton John, 50 Cent, Janice Dickinson and even Dave Ramsey all have one thing in common. At one point during their life they filed for bankruptcy.

Take for example...Nicholas Cage.

Oscar winning actor, Nicholas Cage, is best known for his movies such as *Gone in Sixty Seconds, National Treasure, Snake Eyes, Leaving Las Vegas,* and *The Rock.* At one point Forbes even said he was one of the highest paid actors of all time. He made over $150 million between 1996 and 2011 and it is said he made $40 million in 2009 alone. However, as fast as the money was pouring in, he was spending it even faster. His overspending got out of control with purchases including all sorts of eccentric and extravagant things.

Here are just a few of his purchases:

- dinosaur skulls
- two albino king cobras
- a 40-acre $7 million island in the Bahamas
- the Shah of Iran's $450,000 Lamborghini
- up to 50 other specialty cars, including 9 Rolls Royces and $1 million Ferrari Enzo
- 30 motorcycles
- 4 luxury yachts

...yes it keeps going...

- a famous haunted house in New Orleans
- shrunken pygmy heads
- a 9 foot pyramid tombstone
- expensive high end jewelry
- the first Superman comic

- a crocodile
- a shark
- an octopus
- a private gulf stream jet
- 15 estate homes throughout the world
- 2 European castles
- 50 expensive works of rare art

That is quite the collection! Unfortunately, by 2009 all his overspending caught up to him and he owed the IRS close to $13 million in taxes and was forced to foreclose on several of his properties. He sued his financial manager and was then counter-sued by his financial manager. While he blamed his financial manager, others say it was due to his crazy personal spending. At the end of the day we are responsible for our own finances. He is still struggling to liquidate his assets and fix his finances to this day and continues to take film roles to pay off all of his debts.

I DO NOT want that to happen to you! Ok, maybe I do want you to buy a European castle so I can come visit, but only if you can afford it! Imagine how much truly lasting wealth he could have created with all that money! I mean if he had just lived within his means and stuck to just one mansion he would probably be in a much better situation right now.

I want you to be able to seize any opportunities you are given with your money and create lasting wealth that changes your life in the long term and not just the short term.

I don't really care how much money you make right now. You MUST learn how to live within your means now or you won't be able to hold on to the money you've earned!

One of the most exciting parts of personal finance is learning that by monitoring our income and expenses we have a HUGE opportunity to change our life! It shows us what we are spending our money on so we can decide whether or not that's how we want to spend our money. And once you get this right and know how to live within your means, there is nothing holding you back from becoming a millionaire!

Let's go ahead and dive right into our very first financial statement.

WHAT IS MY *INCOME & EXPENSE STATEMENT*?

The *Income & Expense Statement* summarizes income and expenses over a period of time, usually a month. You can also prepare this statement on a quarterly or yearly basis as well. For our purposes, we will look at all income and expenses from the beginning of the month until the end of the month.

This statement has 2 parts: income & expenses! No surprise there. This is what you need to know:

- Income = cash you earn
- Expenses = cash you spend

Simple, right? Your income minus your expenses equals your positive or negative cash flow. How much money you make minus how much money you spend equals how much money you get to keep for yourself.

Income - Expenses = Cash Flow

If income is greater than your expenses you have positive cash flow and that surplus of cash can be saved or invested. What you do with that extra cash is an equally important part of the equation, but we will dive into that later. If your income is less than your expenses then you have negative cash flow, which you have to find some way to cover.

This negative cash flow, or shortfall in cash, is usually not good and if the shortfall in cash continues month after month, then it can result in taking on a lot of debt, most commonly to your credit card provider. This debt must eventually be paid and over the long term it is not sustainable. When you have several debts piled up over time and owe more than you are earning you are on a troublesome path.

When our income is exactly the same as our expenses that is called "breakeven."

Income = Expenses

When we hover around breakeven with our income and expenses almost equal to each other every month we are living paycheck to paycheck with very little left over to truly improve our financial picture and build wealth. We do not want to fall into the trap of perpetually having our income equal our expenses.

It can be tempting when we get a raise in income to start spending more money to match the new income level but this just leads to a vicious cycle of always trying to "keep up with the Jones,'" which we do not want. We want to break out of the paycheck to paycheck cycle.

Our goal with the income statement is to always have more income and cash coming in than expenses and cash going out.

Income > Expenses

In everyday language that is what we call "living within our means."

This may be obvious but I'm going to go ahead and mention it anyway. When we have more money coming in then going out we ARE living within our means. When we have more money going out then coming in we ARE NOT living within our means.

This is so important because it doesn't really matter how much money you make until you master the art of living within your means. As we've seen with our famous movie stars who go bankrupt, you can have $1MM in income every single month but if you are spending $1.5MM in expenses every month you are not living within your means and you will eventually be in so much debt that you have to file for bankruptcy.

We are going to put together a rough draft of your *Income & Expense Statement* right now. So here is what I want you to do.

Grab your journal, flip to a new page, and at the very top of it write "*INCOME & EXPENSE STATEMENT*" and underline it. Then underneath this title put the date of the previous month end. If today is August 14th then complete your *Income & Expense Statement* as of month end July and write "07/31/21" underneath the title.

Now write "INCOME" at the top of the page, about halfway down the page write "EXPENSES" and at the very bottom of the page write down "CASH FLOW."

It should look something like this.

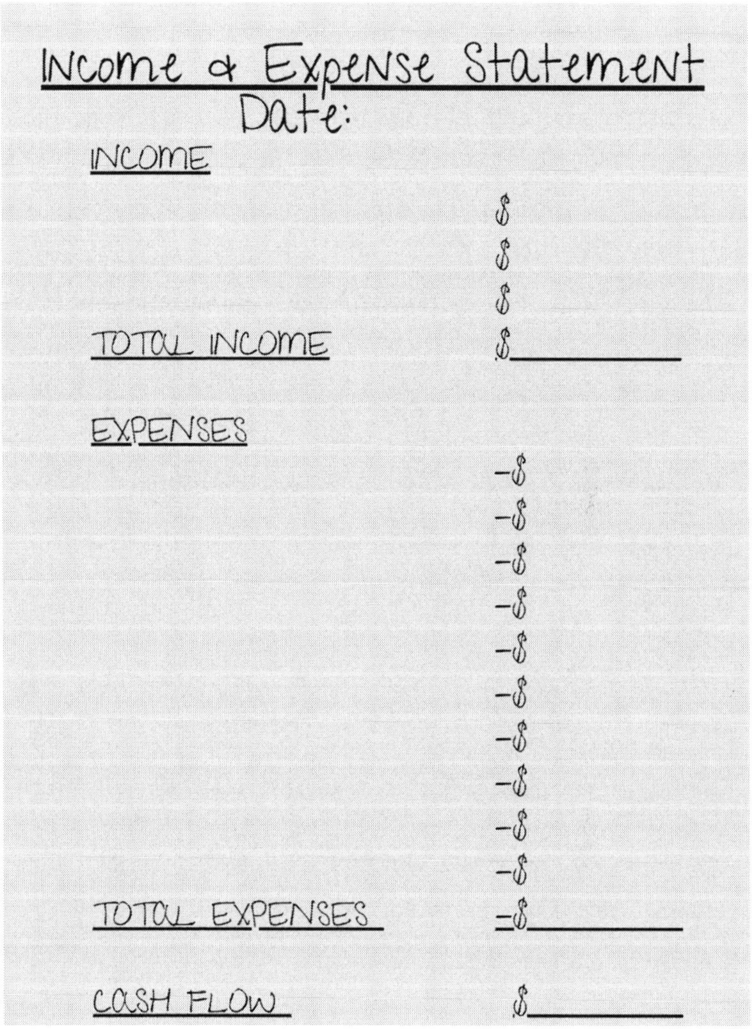
Income & Expense Statement
Date:
INCOME
$
$
$
TOTAL INCOME $______
EXPENSES
-$
-$
-$
-$
-$
-$
-$
-$
-$
-$
TOTAL EXPENSES -$______
CASH FLOW $______

Okay let's go ahead and take a look at our own income and expenses in a little more detail.

HOW MUCH DO I EARN?

I am the Chief Financial Officer (CFO) of my businesses but I am also the CFO of my personal finances as well. And guess what? You are a CFO too! I know it is quite a lofty title but the truth is your finances are your responsibility and you are the CFO of your money and finances. So, start managing your personal finances like the newly promoted CFO you are, Chief.

Could you imagine running a company with no clue how much monthly revenue you are generating and still be able to pay your employees? And yet this is how we have been running our lives! But no more.

Do you know what your annual salary is right off the top of your head? What about how much you are actually taking home every month? Most of us don't.

I remember being pretty sure of my annual salary but then when I sat down to really look at my take home income one day I was shocked that I was bringing home way less after-tax income than I thought I was. By the time taxes and contributions are taken out of our paychecks the after-tax income may look different than the number you have in your head.

Take a moment and think about all the money that you are consistently earning in a given month. Now go to your checking account and confirm what it actually was for the previous month end and then write it down in your journal under the income section. For most people, this is simply your monthly, bi-monthly, or weekly paycheck deposits.

What about pre-tax income vs. after-tax income?

For now, I want you to keep it simple and use after-tax income. Pre-tax income is the amount on your paycheck BEFORE taxes and retirement contributions are taken out. After-tax income is the actual amount of income that is deposited into your checking account each month AFTER any taxes and contributions. We will address any changes to our retirement contributions later on in the book.

What if my income varies throughout the month?

No problem, just look at your bank account and write down what you earned in the past month from the beginning to the end of the month. This doesn't have to be complicated, just identify all current sources of income for the past month and write them down. For most people, this is usually just a few lines.

INCOME	
Bi-monthly salary	$2,200
Bi-monthly salary	$2,200
Birthday check from G-ma	$50
TOTAL INCOME	$4,450

Okay now that you have an idea how much income you are earning let's take a look at the other half of the equation and how much you are spending.

HOW MUCH DO I SPEND?

This is a question I find most people tend to get a little squeamish about. I know it can be uncomfortable to think about but we have to do it.

Again, can you imagine running a business with absolutely no idea of where the business is spending its money? I know for a fact that a business like that will not be in business for very long. Unfortunately, I've seen a lot of really well intentioned business owners go out of business for precisely this reason. Not because their product or service wasn't good, but because they didn't understand their spending and how to change it.

Unless you get a handle on your spending you'll be headed down the same road as those businesses...except the end of the road for you is a mountain of debt, an eviction notice on your door, or filing for bankruptcy.

Okay, that was a little intense. Now shake it off. It doesn't have to be as bad as all that. All we have to do is start looking at where our money is going. Follow the money! That is the first step. Then we will create a *Saving & Spending Plan* later in the book so we can start consciously spending our money on what we want.

"Conscious spending" is simply being aware of where you are spending your money. If you want to improve your financial picture this is a must do!

What we are going to do is take a look at everywhere we are spending our money (checking account, credit card statements, actual cash payments) and categorize our expenses into a few different categories.

You can have as many or as few categories as you would like, it's completely up to you. This is your financial statement and can be 100% customized to you and your life. My rule of thumb is that an expense gets its own category if you are spending more than $100 in it every month. Then lump everything else into an "Other" category.

Common expense categories include:

- Mortgage/Rent
- Student Loan Payments
- Credit Card Payments
- Utilities
- Transportation
- Insurance
- Food & Groceries
- Restaurants & Bars
- Entertainment
- Self-Care & Health
- Personal Development
- Clothing
- Child Care Expenses
- Pet Expenses
- House Expenses
- Car Expenses
- Travel
- Gifts

- Donations
- Other

Trust me, I've pretty much seen the full spectrum of expense categories...for a while, I even had a whole category on my *Income & Expense Statement* just for DoorDash Mexican food! I know, I know, I just REALLY like Mexican food! Chips and queso and a fajita quesadilla...mmm yum!

If you need a separate category for Mexican food too then, by all means, create a separate category for Mexican food. No judgement. Right now we are just trying to get an idea of how much you are spending in different categories each month.

EXPENSES	
Mortgage Loan	-$2,000
Utilities	-$200
Transportation	-$175
Insurance	-$200
Student Loans	-$350
Food	-$480
Entertainment	-$175
Self-Care	-$140
Gifts & Donations	-$155
Other	-$200
TOTAL EXPENSES	-$4,075

The goal is to have an *Income & Expense Statement*

completed so you have a starting point. The important word in that sentence is COMPLETED. I'd rather have it completed than have it be perfect. I don't want this to take you 10 hours because you are trying to make it perfect. Once you have logged into your checking account and credit card accounts you should be able to go through this pretty quickly for the past month. Remember, the goal here is not for this to be perfect on the first go around, it is just to have something to start with. We can always refine it later.

What if my credit card statement is from July 12th - August 11th?

I know that your credit cards are often set up for payments on a weird schedule with statements that don't exactly align with the 1st-31st of the month. I personally find it way easier to review my finances on my own terms, not the weird schedule set by the credit card companies. What I do is look for all the expenses within the past month. So from the first day of the month to the last day of the month. July 1st - July 31st, for example instead of July 12th - August 11th. I know this will feel a little strange at first but it will make tracking your finances and getting everything back on track so much easier.

To find the expenses from the previous month go to the transactions section or account activity section in your account. Look for an option to review all past transactions or all year to date transactions or something similar that will include everything from the previous month. Then simply start with the first expense for July 1st and review all the expenses through July 31st.

Can I just use an online software to do this for me?

Yes, there are some incredible online apps and software that can help with this, but for now, just write your *Income & Expense Statement* out on a piece of paper. Once you can clearly put it together yourself it will be so much easier to learn how to incorporate a financial app or software to help manage this statement going forward. I personally use a free accounting software called Wave to prepare both my personal *Income & Expense Statement* and the other financial statements for my businesses.

HOW'S THE HEALTH OF MY CASH FLOW?

Okay, time to evaluate the health of your cash flow. Let's do the math.

Income - Expenses = Cash Flow.

Do you have positive or negative cash flow?

Income & Expense Statement
7/31/21

INCOME	
Bi-monthly salary	$2,200
Bi-monthly salary	$2,200
Birthday check from G-ma	$50
TOTAL INCOME	$4,450
EXPENSES	
Mortgage Loan	-$2,000
Utilities	-$200
Transportation	-$175
Insurance	-$200
Student Loans	-$350
Food	-$480
Entertainment	-$175
Self-Care	-$140
Gifts & Donations	-$155
Other	-$200
TOTAL EXPENSES	-$4,075
CASH FLOW	$375

Here is an example of an *Income & Expense Statement* with positive cash flow of $375 at the end of the month.

Positive cash flow at the end of each month is an opportunity. With positive cash flow you can begin to put cash towards one of your financial goals.

A few ways you can begin to use your positive cash flow are:

- Save it for an emergency fund
- Save it for a specific large purchase or experience
- Invest it to make more income and generate more cash
- Pay down debt to increase your net worth
- Buy another asset to increase your net worth

Once we get to the point where we are able to consistently generate positive cash flow at the end of each month, things really get interesting and your finances become a lot more fun!

Income & Expense Statement
7/31/21

INCOME	
Bi-monthly salary	$2,200
Bi-monthly salary	$2,200
Birthday check from G-ma	$50
TOTAL INCOME	**$4,450**
EXPENSES	
Mortgage Loan	-$2,500
Utilities	-$250
Transportation	-$175
Insurance	-$245
Student Loans	-$450
Food	-$480
Entertainment	-$375
Self-Care	-$140
Gifts & Donations	-$155
Other	-$440
TOTAL EXPENSES	**-$5,210**
CASH FLOW	**-$760**

Here is an example of an *Income & Expense Statement* with negative cash flow of -$760 at the end of the month.

Negative cash flow at the end of each month is a problem that needs to be fixed. If you have negative cash flow, don't worry, I'm going to help you come up with a *Saving & Spending Plan* later in the book (aka a BUDGET) to begin turning this into positive cash flow at the end of each month. I promise it's not as bad or as hard to do as it may have seemed in the past.

MONEY MOVERS

- Complete your *Income & Expense Statement*.
- Include all after-tax income for the previous month that has gone into your checking account.
- Include all expenses from the 1st - 31st by going to your checking account, credit card accounts, and any other relevant accounts to look up your expenses for the previous month!
- Calculate your cash flow.

DEBT SCHEDULE & CREDIT SCORE

"Rich people use debt to leverage investments and grow cash flows. Poor people use debt to buy things that make rich people richer." - Grant Cardone

DEBT. Ugh I know. Take a deep breath with me, now let it all out. Go grab a glass of wine and settle in. We are going to talk about your debt.

There are thousands of articles out there that talk about credit scores, credit reports and about how to eliminate your debt. Surprisingly though, the financial statement to actually help you understand your debt is way less talked about but it is just as important as your *Income & Expense Statement* and your *Net Worth Statement*. This important financial statement that we all need to know and monitor is our *Debt Schedule*.

But first let's take a little trip down memory lane. Do you remember the first time you were ever offered a credit card? Was it in the mail, at a department store, or on a college campus?

I remember mine...it was in college walking between classes. I was walking along the quad with my fellow classmates at JMU (go Dukes!) on my way to grab lunch at D-hall (grilled cheese Thursdays were the best!). I saw all these booths lined up outside the cafeteria with a bunch of people mulling around. So, naturally, I went over to check it out and realized they were offering credit cards with 0% interest and a free t-shirt. I already had a credit card and decided to pass, but one of my friends Sarah was like, "Yes, sign me up! I could use a good credit card."

Fast forward 4 years later, my friend still has that credit card, but now she has thousands of dollars in debt on the card, that 0% teaser interest rate has ended, and now she is paying something like 26% in interest every month. It happens. That's how they get you.

Credit card lenders will lure you in with their low introductory interest rates and a nice new shiny credit line, but that low interest rate offer eventually expires. And when it does...eeeek. You find yourself with a huge pile of debt, embarrassed, and overwhelmed and unsure of what to do. You just keep making the minimum payment each month, but if you keep heading down that road it could take you years...possibly decades to pay off your debt.

For example, let's say you borrow $8,000 on a credit card with a 17% interest rate and then you never touch the credit card again to buy anything else. If you only make the minimum payment on the card every month, it could take you almost 16 years to pay off your debt! 16 YEARS! And it would cost you another $7,000 extra in interest which is almost as much as you borrowed in the first place. Yikes!

On top of that, you remember the college Sarah and I graduated from? Well it wasn't cheap, and now she also has tens of thousands of dollars in student loan debt too. She wasn't too worried about it in college, because that was a problem for future Sarah to solve, but now that future is here, and it is time to get this sorted out.

And Sarah is not alone. There are millions of other people just like her. According to NerdWallet's 2020 American Household Credit Card Debt Study, the average household owes $6,741 in revolving credit card debt, $28,032 in auto loan debt, $58,468 in student loan debt, and $197,790 in mortgage debt.

We are going to start sorting all this debt out by figuring out our *Debt Schedule.*

Debt is money we are borrowing from someone else. We are paying a lender for the privilege of using their money. This debt or loan will continue to be an expense until the loan or debt has been repaid in full.

There are 2 parts to your payment:

- Principal - the amount of money you are actually borrowing from the lender
- Interest - the amount you are paying to the lender for the privilege of using their money

Think of it this way, when I go to the grocery store to buy a few snacks I am paying $4 for white cheddar popcorn. I pay the store $4, they give me my delicious white cheddar popcorn, and the transaction is complete. I take my white cheddar popcorn home and eat it while watching *Game of Thrones* for the third time. (Yes for the third time, I love that show!) My white cheddar popcorn was a one time expense, I paid for it, and that's that.

But let's say I need $2,000 to buy a couch to lounge on while watching *Game of Thrones,* but I do not have $2,000. I decided to borrow this money and use the line of credit on my American Express credit card which has a 15% interest rate. American Express is the lender, $2,000 is the principal amount I am borrowing from them and they will charge me 15% in interest for every month the balance is outstanding (or not paid back).

If I pay off the full $2,000 balance during the same month that I borrowed the money, I have $0 outstanding and will owe no interest. This is called running a $0 balance on your credit card. If you carry an outstanding balance on your credit card, you will owe interest on that outstanding balance every month.

When I borrow the money on my credit card, unless I pay back that money within 1 month, I have to start paying interest on my borrowed money. In this scenario, I borrowed $2,000 from American Express, they have only loaned it to me and expect me to pay that back. In the meantime, I also owe them 15% interest until I have paid the full $2,000 back, so it is an ongoing transaction instead of a one time transaction, like with the white cheddar popcorn at the store.

My point is when you take out debt you are not just creating a one time expense, you are actually adding an ongoing expense that includes: 1) repayment of the principal and 2) payment of the interest. Plus, since this is not a one time expense, you will be paying it every month until you've paid the full $2,000 balance back on the credit card.

So, if you think my white cheddar popcorn is expensive at $4 a bag, that's nothing compared to how expensive money is!

"Money often costs too much." - Ralph Waldo Emerson

Trust me, I've spent most of my career in lending and I know exactly how the system works, and it works very well. Lenders love to lend you money because they love earning interest on the money they loaned you. They want you to take your time paying it back because the longer you pay them interest the more money they make. And let me be clear, I'm not faulting lenders for that. They are providing you with something you need (more money) and are simply being paid for that service. There is nothing wrong with that. In fact, there are lots of benefits to having lending available and not all people and countries are even given that opportunity. All I'm saying is you need to be well aware of what you are paying for when you obtain a loan.

Some of you might say, "Well, interest rates are low right now, so it's not as expensive." Sure, when interest rates are low, that is when people say, "Money is cheap," because it doesn't cost as much to borrow money from lenders. However, even when interest rates are low that doesn't necessarily mean it is the best time for YOU to borrow money. It completely depends on your current financial picture.

Even when interest rates are low, just remember, you are paying for the privilege to use someone else's money and that privilege creates an ongoing expense for you every single month.

Now don't get me wrong, there is a time and place to borrow money and take on more leverage. Not all debt is bad debt, and it is important to understand the difference.

Loans are sometimes referred to as leverage because you are leveraging someone else's money and this can be really great, when used appropriately, and is a huge part of the reason we have such a thriving capitalist society.

I personally use leverage to grow my net worth when purchasing additional real estate property. However, I know what my financial picture looks like and I know that I am able to comfortably manage those loans.

A good rule of thumb is that if you are taking out a loan for consumption or to spend on items that will increase your expenses or your liabilities then it is a bad idea. If you are considering a loan to invest in something that will help you generate income or will increase your assets it may be a good idea.

For example, borrowing money from a lender to purchase an investment property that generates cash flow and increases your assets: Good debt

Online shopping on a credit card for clothes or electronics that you don't have the money to pay for, which will increase your liabilities: Bad debt.

When it comes to your personal finances, I just want you to understand exactly what you are getting into when you acquire more debt. You are borrowing someone else's money and you are paying for that privilege.

I want you to go in with eye's wide open when you borrow money and have a clear plan for how you will repay the money you have borrowed. If you don't have the cash to pay for the product or service, then think twice about if you really need it.

Okay what if things have already gotten a little out of hand and you aren't sure how much debt you currently have? Where do you start?

WHAT IS MY *DEBT SCHEDULE*?

You start by compiling your *Debt Schedule*. There are 2 components to your *Debt Schedule* and those are:

- Credit Score
- Loan Information

You want to know your current credit score(s) as well as all of the information about your existing loans. So, grab your journal again and let's set up the *Debt Schedule*. At the top of the page we are going to put "*DEBT SCHEDULE*" as our title and underline it with the current date right below the title. Then we will include our current credit score(s) next. And lastly we will include all the details we need to know about our current loans.

The information you will want to have for your current loans includes:

- Lender
- Loan Type
- Outstanding Loan Balance
- Interest Rate
- Maturity Date
- Payment Amount

Here is an example of what you want your Debt Schedule to look like.

Debt Schedule
Date:

Credit Scores:

Lender	Type	Loan Balance	Interest	Maturity	Payment
TOTAL					

WHAT IS MY CREDIT SCORE?

Your first stop is to determine your credit score. Your credit score is an important part of your financial picture. Your credit score is the number that lenders use to assess how credit worthy you are and if they can trust you to pay back your debts in a timely fashion.

Think of your credit score as the GPA for your debt. It is a number between 300 and 850 that is calculated on several factors including your payment history, credit inquiries, credit usage, length of credit history, and any new credit you have. The higher your credit score the better interest rate a lender will give you when you apply for a loan. The goal is to have as high a credit score as possible.

If you apply for a loan and have a low credit score at the time, there is a good chance you'll be denied. If you are approved with your low credit score, you can expect a very high interest rate, because the lender is taking more risk to loan you money, so they will charge you more for that.

On the flip side, if you have a high credit score, you are a more attractive borrower and lenders will give you a lower interest rate. Lenders are funny like that. When you are broke and need the money, they don't want to lend it to you and will charge you more for it. When you are rich and don't need the money as much, they want to lend it to you and will charge you less for it.

Improve your credit score and use it to your advantage instead of letting it become a disadvantage.

Okay, where to find your credit score...there are so many places! Technically, you have three credit scores from the three credit reporting agencies: Experian, Equifax, and TransUnion. You can go to each of them to pull your three credit scores.

My favorite app to easily keep track of my credit score is Experian because I can see my Experian, Equifax, and TransUnion credit scores all in one place while also being able to review my Experian credit report as well. You are entitled to one free credit report from each credit reporting agency every year. When you pull the credit reports from Equifax and TransUnion you can review those in the app as well. You can upgrade your account to pull all 3 credit reports monthly, however, you don't need to and can just use the free basic plan to access all the information you need. To check your credit score in this app only takes a minute or so and to review the credit report is just a few minutes.

There are lots of credit monitoring websites out there as well where you can pull one or more of your credit scores for free. These will give you a good idea of what your score is and are useful to monitor any changes to your credit score over time.

A few that you can check out are:

- Credit Karma
- Credit Sesame
- Credit.com
- Wallet Hub
- Nerd Wallet
- Credit Wise

Many credit card companies will offer their customers a free look at their credit score as well. And don't worry, checking your own credit score won't lower it.

Your credit score only takes a slight dip when a lender does a "hard pull." This usually happens when you apply for a new credit card or loan. The credit score usually bounces back in the next couple of months, so it's not something you need to stress over, but you also don't want to be applying for credit cards and loans all of the time.

You will also hear the term "soft pull" used, which is

where a lender will take a look at your creditworthiness by pulling your credit history without it affecting your credit score.

What exactly does a good credit score look like?

According to FICO credit score ranges:

- Excellent: 800 - 850
- Very good: 740 - 799
- Good: 670 - 739
- Fair: 580 - 669
- Very Poor: 300 - 579

According to VantageScore credit score ranges:

- Excellent: 781 - 850
- Good: 661 - 780
- Fair: 601 - 660
- Poor: 500 - 600
- Very Poor: 300 - 499

If your lender is pulling from Experian they will see your FICO credit score. If your lender is pulling from TransUnion they will see your VantageScore credit score.

Bottom line - your goal is to be in the 700 or 800s and the higher your score the better.

If you aren't quite there yet, don't worry, there are a few things you can do to improve your credit score.

1. **Start paying your bills on time** - For your

credit score to change you'll need at least 6 months of on-time payments.

2. **Increase your credit line and don't max it out** - I know this one sounds a bit counterintuitive, but there is this thing called your credit utilization rate. It's just a percentage of the total credit line that you are using. Lenders don't like to see you completely maxing out your credit line. So, if you increase your credit line, and keep the balance low, it will improve your credit utilization rate. Simply call your credit card company and ask for a credit increase. If your account is in good standing, they should grant your request. Just because you have access to a higher credit line does NOT mean you need to use it. Do not max out your credit line. Be smart people.
3. **Don't close out old credit card accounts** - If you are no longer using an old credit card you are better off leaving the account open than actually closing the account. This is for two reasons. First, because keeping it open improves your credit utilization rate. Second, because you lose any good credit history you built up when you close out the card. If the credit card has an annual membership fee, call the credit card company and ask to downgrade the card to one they offer that doesn't have an annual fee. That does not mean you cancel the card and open

one that doesn't have a fee. This means asking them to downgrade the current credit card and all of its glorious history of on time payments, to one that doesn't have a fee.

Overall, knowing your credit score tells you and lenders just how credit worthy you are and improving your credit score takes you one step closer to improving your financial picture.

This little debt GPA of yours can affect you more over the course of your lifetime than all of your grades from high school and college combined. Your credit score is the one number that can either cost or save you a lot of money. Make sure you use it to your advantage so you have access to more opportunities to borrow if you ever want to.

HOW DO I PULL MY CREDIT REPORT?

Your next stop to find information about your debt should be your credit report. Your credit report will include debts like your credit cards, student loans, car loans, mortgages, and more. The credit report will have the amounts you owe on each loan along with your payment history and any delinquencies.

If you haven't pulled one in a long time and are scared of what you will find, I know it can be scary, but I promise it is the right thing to do. Besides, it can't really get any worse than it is right now, there is only room for improvement so you might as well take a little peek.

I know it can be confusing trying to pull your credit report but here is what you need to know. Under federal law you can obtain one FREE credit report every 12 months by visiting AnnualCreditReport.com.

There are three major credit bureaus to pull your report from: Experian, Equifax, and TransUnion. You can also usually pull your credit report directly on each of the Experian, Equifax, or TransUnion websites. How it works is the companies you owe money to report your debt balances to these three reporting agencies, which then compile the information into your credit report.

Should I order all three reports at once?

You can, but you don't have to. The answer depends on your situation. If you are about to purchase something big like a new car or a home then you may want to get all three reports at once. That way you can see everything a lender would see and start improving your credit right away.

However, if you are not planning a large purchase and are just trying to get an idea of your current credit history, requesting just one at first or each of them over time might be a better choice. When you spread them out, you can watch for expected changes or suspicious activity throughout the year.

Whichever strategy you choose, mark your calendar so you know when you can request your next free credit report.

Next it is time to dig into each loan. Once you have your credit report in front of you, review each and every loan that is reported. For each loan on the report you will want to go to that lender's website directly to access your current loan information.

On each lender's website you can see the current outstanding loan balance that you owe, the interest rate, the maturity date, and the other loan terms. If you don't have online access, you may have to call the loan company directly. You can usually find a phone number for the loan company with a quick Google search. Be ready to provide your loan account number if you see it on the credit report. Otherwise, the customer service representative can usually find your account with your social security number.

Your credit report includes most of your loans, however, any medical debt, personal loans from family and friends, or retailer debt may not be included on your credit report if it hasn't reached a collections office yet. That is why it is important for you to compile your own *Debt Schedule* to ensure you are including everything you currently owe.

WHAT DO MY LOANS LOOK LIKE?

When compiling your *Debt Schedule* there are several bits of information you want to know about your loan.

- Who you owe money to - lender

- What type of loan it is - loan type
- How much you still owe them - outstanding loan balance
- How much it is costing you - interest rate
- When you have to pay it back - maturity date
- Current monthly payment amount - minimum loan payment

Each of these is an important piece of your *Debt Schedule*. To compile your *Debt Schedule* you need to look up each and every one of your loans and find this information.

In case you need a reminder, these debts or loans may include:

- Credit card lines of credit
- Mortgage loans
- Student loans
- Auto loans
- Equity lines of credit
- Personal loans
- Other loans

Here is an example of what a *Debt Schedule* would look like:

Debt Schedule
7/31/21

Credit Scores: 765, 774, 769

Lender & Type	Loan Balance	Interest	Maturity	Payment
Amex: CC	$4,500	25.5%	10/01/21	$175
Chase: CC	$6,500	18.4%	05/31/22	$220
Fannie Mae: College	$9,000	4.3%	05/30/25	$245
Toyota: Car	$20,500	9.5%	09/30/27	$540
Wells Fargo: Mtg	$380,000	4.2%	08/22/48	$1,850
Mom & Dad: Personal	$2,500	0%	TBD	$100
TOTAL	$423,000			$3,130

For right now, I just want you to compile your *Debt Schedule* so you know how much debt you have. Don't worry about what to do with this information quite yet. In chapter 7 we will actually take this information and begin working on your *Debt Payoff Plan* so you can begin reducing your debt. But for right now I just want you to compile all the information by filling out your *Debt Schedule*.

The good news is once you've put your *Debt Schedule* together the first time it is a lot easier each month because now you know where to find all your loan information.

MONEY MOVERS

- Pull at least one of your credit scores from any of the credit monitoring websites or the credit bureaus and write it down. Begin tracking your credit score on a consistent basis.
- Access your free annual credit report on AnnualCreditReport.com or from one of the 3 credit bureaus (Experian, Equifax, TransUnion).
- Complete your *Debt Schedule*. Include your credit score(s). Log into each lender's website to find your loan information and fill in the lender, loan type, loan balance, interest rate, maturity date, and payment amount with one row for each loan.
- Total up all of your loan balances and all of your monthly loan payments.

NET WORTH STATEMENT

"Wealth is not about having a lot of money, it is about having a lot of options." - Chris Rock

Next it is time to dive into the *Net Worth Statement*. Net worth is what people are referencing when they are like, "Oh yes, Sally sold her business and is now worth $1MM."

"I heard Steve got in early with crypto and is currently worth $4MM."

It is Steve and Sally's net worth that is being referenced and this chapter is where you get to discover yours.

The true measure of a person's wealth is their net worth...not their income.

Did you catch that? Let me repeat that…it's your net worth, not your income, that determines how rich you are!

Let me rephrase that…it DOES NOT matter how

much you make in income, it is how much you keep that matters when it comes to building wealth! That means that every single one of you can become rich regardless of your current income level.

I'm giving you the answer to the age old question - how do I get rich?

Everyone seems to think you need more money to get rich and although more money will indeed help expedite how fast you get rich. The answer to, "How do I get rich?" is not make more money.

The answer to, "How do I get rich?" is to keep your money and grow your net worth.

You can actually have someone with a lower income have a higher net worth than someone with a higher income if they know how to manage their cash flow and debt better.

Take Laurie for example who is a teacher and makes $44,000 a year and has positive cash flow every month and has been able to consistently save and invest her money so she now has an $84,000 net worth.

Robert is an insurance agent and makes $88,000 a year with positive cash flow every month and now has a $11,000 net worth.

Rebecca is a software engineer makes $122,000 a year with positive cash flow every month and has a $1.2MM net worth.

FYI, that example with Rebecca is your secret millionaire next door neighbor, although you probably wouldn't have guessed it because she drives a Honda Civic and shops at Target.

Unfortunately, the same can be true on the flip side as well. You can have someone like our friend Nicholas Cage with a very high income, who hasn't figured out how to manage their cash flow, and has taken on too much debt who has a very low or negative net worth.

Anthony, a famous basketball player, who makes $1.4MM a year but is living outside his means with negative cash flow every month. He continues to take on more and more credit card debt buying new cars, throwing parties, and eating out at fancy restaurants. Eventually, his debtors refuse to lend him anymore and he declares bankruptcy with -$661,000 net worth.

Dalia, a dental hygienist, who makes $143,000 a year but has negative cash flow every month, very high student loans, a large mortgage loan and other debts has -$37,000 net worth.

Andrea, a retail store manager, who makes $75,000 a year is living paycheck to paycheck and just can't seem to pull herself out of the negative cycle of debt with -$42,000 net worth.

My point is, it is possible for both high earners and low earners to have negative net worth if they overspend and take on too much debt. We traditionally associate the words rich or poor with income levels, but in truth you are either rich or poor based on your net worth and how much of your money you are able to keep. It is possible for those who make a lot of money to actually be very poor and those who don't make as much money to be very rich.

I just want you to know that how rich you become is not dependent on how much money you currently make…and YOU CAN become very very wealthy with a high net worth regardless of your current income! Then, I want you to help your friends and family become very wealthy too, so we can pass on generational wealth, financial knowledge, and make even more positive changes in this beautiful world we've been given.

Okay...thanks for sticking with me there...I just am really passionate about it because this is one of the most common misconceptions I see when it comes to your finances! I'll step off my soapbox now and we can get down to it.

WHAT IS MY *NET WORTH STATEMENT*?

Your *Net Worth Statement* is a financial snapshot that shows your financial wealth at a specific point in time.

Your *Net Worth Statement* is made up of 2 components:

- Assets - things you own
- Liabilities - debts you owe

Assets are things you own that have value and can be turned into cash. Liabilities are debts you owe to others and create expenses. When you take your assets and subtract your liabilities you are left with your net worth.

Assets - Liabilities = Net Worth[1]

If your assets are greater than your liabilities you have positive net worth and if your assets are less than your liabilities you have negative net worth. As you can imagine, our goal is to have our assets greater than our liabilities and to continue to increase our net worth and therefore our wealth every month.

Assets > Liabilities

For some, the reality is that you might have a negative net worth. It is okay to start with a negative net worth, it is not the end of the world. If this is you, do not worry, you are not alone and my entire goal with this book is to help you change that. I've seen so many determined people change their net worth and I know that you can too!

Okay, I want you to put together your *Net Worth Statement*. Grab that journal again and at the top of the page I want you to title it "*NET WORTH STATEMENT*" and include the current date. Under the title write "ASSETS" and in the middle of the page write "LIABILITIES." Then at the bottom of the page write "NET WORTH." It should look a little something like this.

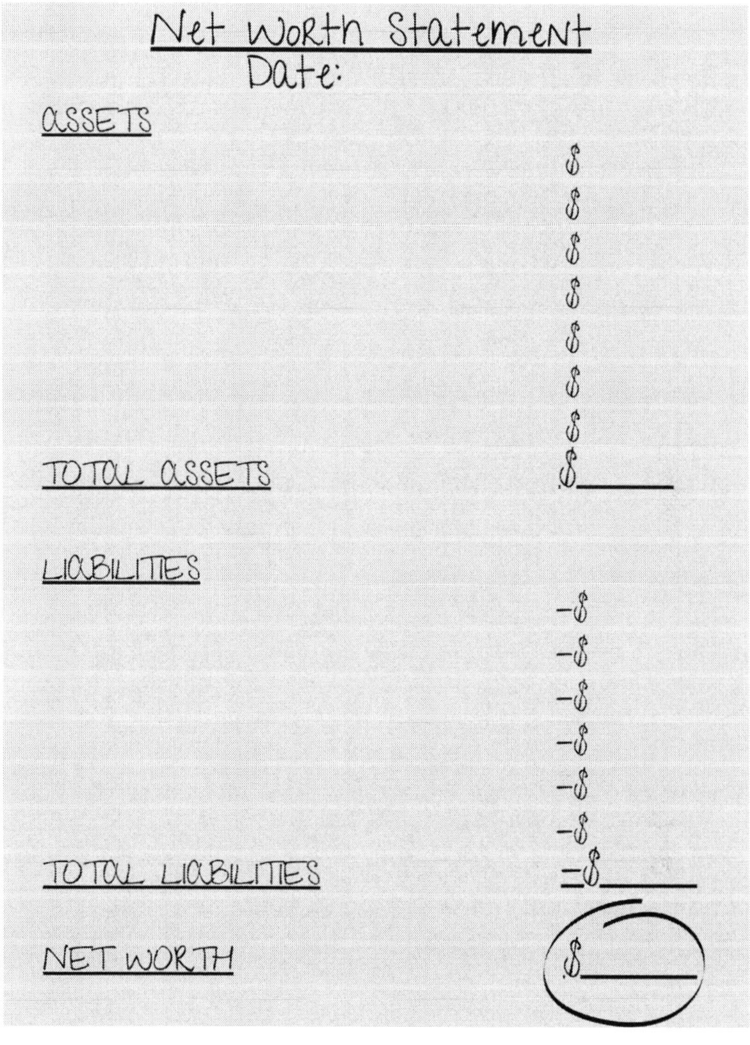

HOW MUCH DO I OWN?

First, we are going to take a look at your assets, or everything you own, that have value and could be sold for cash.

We often think of assets in 2 categories:

- Liquid assets
- Illiquid assets

Liquid assets are those that can be quickly turned into cash, usually within 24-48 hours, such as the money in your checking account. The total of your liquid assets tells you how well prepared you are for a financial emergency or loss of income in case you need to quickly get your hands on some cash. Your liquid assets are also the first items you put away when your shifty cousin Joey Soft-hands comes over for the holidays looking for something to pawn.

Liquid assets include:

- Cash
- Checking account balance
- Savings account balance
- Money market account balance
- Short term investments - stocks, bonds, ETFs, mutual funds, listed commodities, cryptocurrencies
- Cash surrender value of life insurance[2]

Illiquid assets are the assets that would take longer to turn into cash such as your home, retirement accounts or long-term investments, which could take several weeks or months to liquidate. Let's take your home for example, although this has significant value, you would need time to find a realtor, get the house ready for sale, list it on the

MLS, negotiate with a buyer, set a closing date, move out, and finalize the sale of the home to turn it into spendable cash. While that might be a sizable check at the closing table, it isn't cash you can access quickly or could rely on in a pinch.

Illiquid assets include:

- Retirement accounts - 401K, 403B, IRA
- Tax-advantaged accounts - HSA, 529 plan
- Real estate property - primary residence, vacation home, investment properties
- Long term investments - certificate of deposit, hedge funds, private equity funds, fixed income annuities
- Business equity - the equity value in a business you own[3]
- Vehicles - car, truck, boat, motorcycle[4]
- Other personal property - jewelry, art, furnishings

Another important thing to note is the difference between appreciating assets and depreciating assets. There are some assets on our *Net Worth Statement* that appreciate, or gain value, over time such as our house. Other assets on our *Net Worth Statement* depreciate, or lose value, over time such as our car.

Appreciating asset = goes up in price over time
Depreciating asset = goes down in price over time

If you expect to be able to sell the asset for more than what you bought it for, it is an appreciating asset. We want to invest in appreciating assets and minimize our purchase of depreciating assets.

Appreciating assets:

- Real estate
- Land
- Stocks
- Cryptocurrency
- Precious metals - high quality gold, silver and gemstones
- Collectors items - vintage cars, rare art, fine wine, watches
- Businesses

Depreciating assets include:

- Vehicles - car, truck, boat, motorcycle
- Personal property - jewelry, furniture
- Electronics - computers, phones

Now we can't always know for sure that a specific asset will appreciate but in general there are certain asset classes that do tend to appreciate over time. A single stock, for example, will go up in price over time when the underlying business is doing well. We can't know for sure that one particular stock will succeed and appreciate over time, however, the stock market as a whole has historically gone up over time. So, if you diversify and invest in multiple stocks then you will see that your overall investment portfolio will usually appreciate with time.

Real estate is another asset class that historically goes up in price over time. There are exceptions, but overall the real estate market as a whole has continued to have price increases over time. Real estate is one of many investors' favorite appreciating asset classes. In fact, owning real estate is also a tax-advantaged investment, which I won't go into detail on right now, but in short the IRS has created tax code where it is in your favor to own real estate and it is a really great asset for you to invest in.

Now for some of the depreciating assets. Your car is almost always a depreciating asset. As soon as you buy your car and drive it off the lot it loses value. Don't believe me? Just go to Kelly Blue Book and look up the price of a 1 year old car compared to the price to buy a brand new car from the same manufacturer. Cars, boats, motorcycles, trucks, and most other vehicles lose value quickly and could only be sold for less than what they were originally purchased for. The only exceptions are super rare or vintage cars that could be sold for more than they were originally bought for because a special collectors market for those cars exists.

The same thing applies for your jewelry, furniture, or cell phones. Take a look at any of the secondary markets for these on Craigslist or Ebay and you will notice an immediate drop in price. You will almost always have to sell these items for less than what you bought them for.

The reason I say this is because sometimes we think these depreciating assets may be worth more than they actually are.

For example, after my divorce I was shocked when I went to sell my diamond ring. At the time, I thought diamonds were an appreciating asset. After I got divorced, I thought I would surely get more or at least the same price for my ring as when it was purchased because I thought diamonds go up in price over time. Boy, was I surprised. Not only did I not get even close to the same price as what my ring was bought for, I also discovered the secondary market for diamonds was very different then I thought. The truth is other people do not value your diamond ring the same way you do and there isn't a strong secondary market for engagement rings. Jewelry sellers may be able to use the diamonds from it, but you don't see many couples in a secondary market buying used engagement rings. Sorry to burst your bubble, but your diamond ring is a depreciating asset. The only exception to this is with very rare and precious gemstones, which the majority of people do not own.

Whenever you are thinking about buying your next asset just ask yourself the question, "Do I think this asset will go up in value and could I sell it for more than I bought it for?" If yes, fantastic, go for it. If no, maybe rethink if you want to purchase that depreciating asset.

You want to become wealthy, right? Hint - rich people invest in appreciating assets.

HOW MUCH DO I OWE OTHERS?

Now we will take a look at your liabilities which are all of the loans, debts, and obligations you owe to other people.

We think about our liabilities in 2 categories:

- Short term liabilities
- Long term liabilities

Short term liabilities also known as "current liabilities" are loans or debts that you owe in the short term, usually within 1 year or less, such as credit card loans.

Long term liabilities are loans or debts that you owe with a longer loan term, usually over 1 year, such as a 30 year mortgage loan.

Short term liabilities include:

- Credit card lines of credit
- Taxes owed
- Unpaid bills

Long term liabilities include:

- Mortgage loans
- Student loans
- Vehicle loans
- Home equity lines of credit (HELOC)
- Alimony/child support
- Personal loans - from family or friends

- Other loans

Your liabilities should be fairly easy to put together because we have all the information already compiled on our *Debt Schedule*. Just flip back to your *Debt Schedule* to compile your liabilities.

For all of the liabilities on your *Net Worth Statement* we are only going to include the outstanding loan balance from each debt, not the monthly payment amount. We want to look at how much total debt you have so your total liabilities on the *Net Worth Statement* should be the same amount as the total outstanding loan balances from your *Debt Schedule*.

Lender & Type	Loan Balance	Interest	Maturity	Payment
Amex: CC	$4,500	25.5%	10/01/21	$175
Chase: CC	$6,500	18.4%	05/31/22	$220
Fannie Mae: College	$9,000	4.3%	05/30/25	$245
Toyota: Car	$20,500	9.5%	09/30/27	$540
Wells Fargo: Mtg	$380,000	4.2%	08/22/48	$1,850
Mom & Dad: Personal	$2,500	0%	TBD	$100
TOTAL	$423,000			$3,130

LIABILITIES	
Chase Credit Card Balance	-$6,500
AmEx Credit Card Balance	-$4,500
Mortgage Loan	-$380,000
Student Loans	-$9,000
Car Loan	-$20,500
Personal Loan	-$2,500
TOTAL LIABILITIES	-$423,000

Let's say you have a mortgage loan with a $1,850 a month payment and a total outstanding loan balance of $380,000. I want you to include the $380,000 as the liability on your *Net Worth Statement*.

If you have a $10,000 credit card line of credit, with current outstanding balance of $4,500, and minimum monthly payment of $175 a month. I want you to include the $4,500 as the liability on your *Net Worth Statement*.

Then total up all of your loan balances for the month for the total liabilities. The total loan balance from your *Debt Schedule* and total liabilities from your *Net Worth Statement* should match.

HOW RICH OR POOR AM I?

Okay, moment of truth, let's calculate your net worth with some simple math and figure out how rich or poor you currently are. Here is the formula, take your total assets minus your total liabilities and you have your positive or negative net worth.

Assets - Liabilities = Net Worth

Here is an example of a *Net Worth Statement* with a positive net worth.

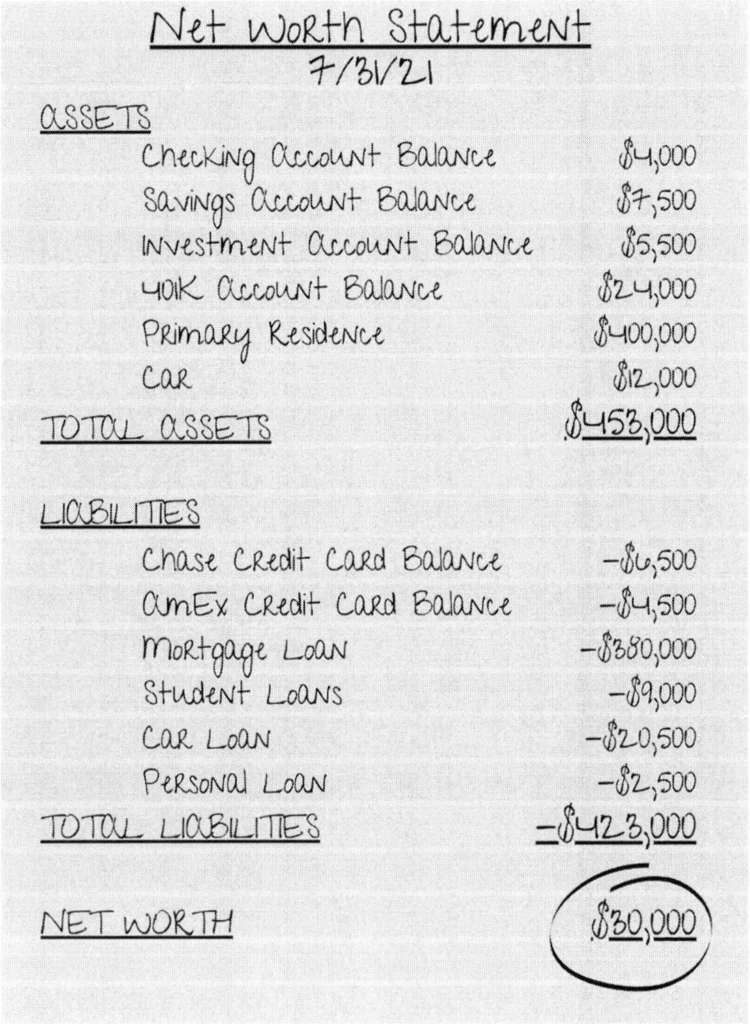

Net Worth Statement
7/31/21

ASSETS	
Checking Account Balance	$4,000
Savings Account Balance	$7,500
Investment Account Balance	$5,500
401K Account Balance	$24,000
Primary Residence	$400,000
Car	$12,000
TOTAL ASSETS	$453,000
LIABILITIES	
Chase Credit Card Balance	-$6,500
AmEx Credit Card Balance	-$4,500
Mortgage Loan	-$380,000
Student Loans	-$9,000
Car Loan	-$20,500
Personal Loan	-$2,500
TOTAL LIABILITIES	-$423,000
NET WORTH	$30,000

Here is an example of a *Net Worth Statement* with a

negative net worth.

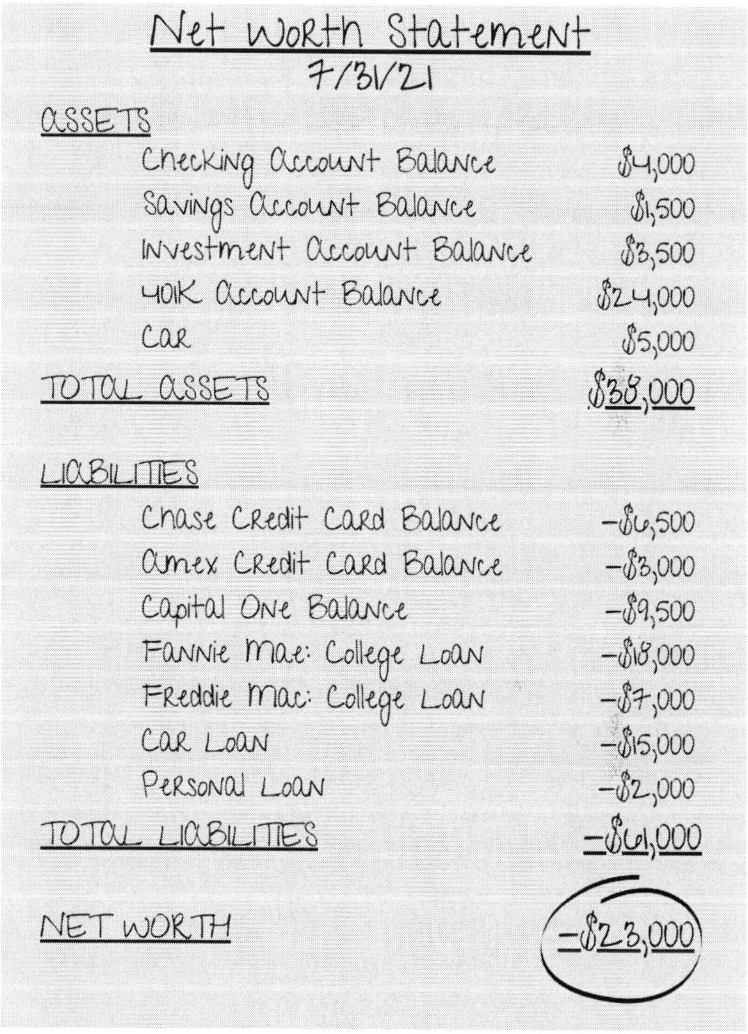

Net Worth Statement
7/31/21

ASSETS		
	Checking Account Balance	$4,000
	Savings Account Balance	$1,500
	Investment Account Balance	$3,500
	401K Account Balance	$24,000
	Car	$5,000
TOTAL ASSETS		$38,000
LIABILITIES		
	Chase Credit Card Balance	-$6,500
	Amex Credit Card Balance	-$3,000
	Capital One Balance	-$9,500
	Fannie Mae: College Loan	-$18,000
	Freddie Mac: College Loan	-$7,000
	Car Loan	-$15,000
	Personal Loan	-$2,000
TOTAL LIABILITIES		-$61,000
NET WORTH		-$23,000

The first time you calculate your net worth can be a bit shocking...either as a good surprise or a bad surprise. If you've only ever relied on looking at your checking account balance to determine how wealthy you feel, I can understand the shock of seeing your true net worth.

If it is a pleasant surprise, woohoo, congrats!!! Kudos to you, pop some champagne and let's celebrate!

If it is an unpleasant surprise, and your net worth is negative, don't be too discouraged. Although I know a negative number is not fun to see I am still very proud of you because at least now you know. Take consolation knowing that lots and lots of people have been where you are right now and have climbed up out of that hole and on to financial freedom!

The true power of compiling your *Net Worth Statement* is not whether your net worth number is positive or negative. The power is in the awareness of what it is and the knowledge that you have the ability to change it. You can begin to track it and ensure that it is improving over time and slowly but surely watch as your net worth moves in the right direction towards more and more wealth.

Okay, now that you've done it once the question I usually get is, "How often should I calculate my net worth?" My answer, "As often as you want."

You could calculate your net worth every day if you wanted. Usually you won't see much of a change day to day, so starting out I recommend reviewing it once a week. That way you can get into the habit of checking it and start noticing how it is changing. However, once you get the hang of it, I recommend calculating it once a month to have your *Net Worth Statement* coincide with when you prepare your *Income & Expense Statement* and

Debt Schedule. I calculate my net worth on the 1st of every month.

Once you begin tracking your net worth you will start to notice patterns. You will be able to identify where to focus your efforts in order to continue building your wealth on the path to your financial freedom. And, if you follow the guidance in this book, you will be able to see your assets increase and your liabilities decrease each and every month.

MONEY MOVERS

- Complete your *Net Worth Statement*.
- In the assets section write down all of your liquid and illiquid assets.
- In the liabilities section write down all of your short term and long term liabilities.
- Then take your total assets and subtract your total liabilities and write down your total net worth at the bottom of the page.

A QUICK MESSAGE FROM JESSICA

Hi there! Are you enjoying the book so far? I'd love to hear your thoughts!

Many readers do not know how hard reviews are to come by, and how much they help indie authors out.

I would be incredibly grateful if you could take just 60 seconds to write a brief review on Amazon, even if it's just a few sentences!

Thank you so much for taking the time to share your thoughts! Your review will genuinely make a difference for me and help gain exposure for my work!

PART II
FUTURE FINANCIAL CONDITION

"Alice: Would you tell me, please, which way I ought to go from here?
The Cheshire Cat: That depends a good deal on where you want to get to.
Alice: I don't much care where.
The Cheshire Cat: Then it doesn't much matter which way you go." - Lewis Carrol

Congrats! You now have a great understanding of your current financial condition. Now that you know where you are starting from, the second half of this book is all about understanding where you want to go. After all, it is a lot easier to reach a destination if you know where you want to go. For example, on a road trip it's a lot more likely you will make it to Nashville, TN if at the beginning of your trip you know you are trying to get to Nashville. Otherwise, who knows where you might end up. It could be a cool place, but it most likely won't be Nashville. It is the same with our finances. This half of the book is all about identifying where you want to go and coming up with your roadmap to get there. Safe travels.

WHAT DO YOU REALLY WANT?

"So tell me what you want, what you really, really want. I'll tell you what I want, what I really, really want." - Spice Girls

You are doing great! You now have all three of your personal financial statements prepared. That is huge and I'm so proud of you.

However, what if you don't like what you see on your financial statements?

That's okay.

It's perfectly normal. Everyone starts somewhere and this is just the beginning of your financial journey so it will only get better from here.

Here's the thing though. It's really hard to cut back on your spending or change your finances without a very good reason to. So, the question becomes what do you really want?

Let's take a minute, take a deep breath, and really think

about what you actually want to do with your money and your finances. Why are you doing all of this? Why improve your finances?

It's a lot easier cutting back on your spending, getting rid of your debt, and setting up a savings plan if you know exactly what you are trying to achieve and why it is so important for you to achieve it.

We often buy products or services based on what we are marketed to at the moment. We make reactionary purchases and don't always stop to really think about what we truly value and want to spend our money on. For example, my fiancé has never gone to Costco without making at least one impulse purchase. Although this is perfectly natural, and what marketing and advertising departments are counting on, I'd rather be the boss of my money and decide when, where, and how I want to spend it myself.

To do that we need to figure out what our financial values and goals look like so that we know what we really want to spend our money on and can ensure our spending is in alignment with our values and goals.

WHAT DO YOU VALUE?

What do I mean when I say financial values? Why is it important to understand your current financial values and how they are impacting your life?

Well, your personal values are what drive you forward and shape your life. They determine the goals you set. The decisions you make. The people you help. The products you want. The person you become. The things you do.

Your values and goals drive your behaviors, which include how you decide to spend your time and money. It feels good to align with your values and it can feel terrible to go against them.

Values are the things you hold dear and consider to be important. They are very personal and differ from person to person. Your current values come from a variety of sources including your childhood experiences, your parents, other role models, your peers, advertising, social media, and life experiences. They are shaped by the culture you've grown up in and the beliefs you've formed. They can be personal qualities (such as loyalty), broad categories (like relationships), as well as material things (like cars).

Just take a look at what you spend your time and money on the most and you'll have a pretty good idea of what you have been valuing the most. Sometimes we can be surprised at what we are placing a lot of value on and realize it is not really what we want to be spending our money on.

"Don't tell me where your priorities are. Show me where you spend your money and I'll tell you what they are." - James W. Frick

---

How you spend, save, or invest your money is a direct reflection of what you are currently placing value on, whether intentional or not. That includes when you are NOT spending, NOT saving, or NOT investing as well. All of these are decisions you make with your money and impact your life.

Keep in mind although you may have a certain set of values right now, as we go through life our experiences and values can change and something that once seemed important may lose priority.

For example, a lot of people find that their values will change when they become parents and all of a sudden their value for family becomes a very high priority. It is natural for your values to change, which is why it is important to check in every once and a while to see if you are still living, spending, saving, and investing according to your current values.

You see, what we value in life actually influences the goals that we set for ourselves. Our goals are really just an extension of our current personal values. Once we have goals to strive for, we can then determine the tactics or strategies we need to reach them.

When setting financial goals, the most effective and efficient way to ensure success is to first understand your values, second set your goals, and third determine the strategy to accomplish your goals.

1. Understand your values
2. Set your goals

3. Determine your strategy

If you try to determine your strategy first before you understand your values, you will find it difficult to apply that strategy and stick to it in the long run. Have you ever tried to stick to a budget before and failed? Chances are you tried cutting expenses before understanding your values and goals and so your budget cuts didn't align with what you really wanted.

To help understand the relationship between your values and your goals I've included common financial values with examples of financial goals someone with those values may have:

Value - Security

- Goal: set up an emergency fund
- Goal: have enough money for retirement

Value - Freedom

- Goal: achieve financial independence with additional income streams
- Goal: pay off all credit card debt and be debt free

Value - Travel & Adventure

- Goal: take a big trip or vacation every quarter

Value - Home Life

- Goal: save for a down payment to buy a house
- Goal: renovate and improve the kitchen

Value - Family

- Goal: pay for a great school for my children's education
- Goal: build generational wealth for my children

Value - Health

- Goal: pay for a gym membership every month
- Goal: buy healthy food and fresh produce

Value - Giving

- Goal: give to an organization I care about every month

Value - Education

- Goal: attend personal and professional development conferences
- Goal: read a new book every month

Value - Entertainment

- Goal: enjoy going out to nice restaurants and bars
- Goal: attend live concerts of my favorite artists

Value - Relaxation

- Goal: join a yoga studio
- Goal: enjoy a spa once a month

You really can have anything you want in life… true...but we need to be a little bit more specific. You have to prioritize what you want based on what you value. Time is a limited resource and we only have so much of it in one lifetime.

You really can have anything you want that you value…as long as you prioritize it in your life. Your values will help you set and prioritize your financial goals so that you can address the most important aspects of your life (according to you) first.

Here are some other values to consider including the ones mentioned above:

Achievement, Adventure, Appearance, Celebration, Cleanliness, Connection, Creativity, Education, Entertainment, Fairness, Family, Freedom, Friends, Fun, Growth, Giving, Happiness, Health, Hobbies, Home Life, Honesty, Independence, Integrity, Investing, Love, Loyalty, Marriage, Music, Peace, Power, Relationships, Relaxation, Religion, Socializing, Spirituality, Sports,

Security, Self Care, Stability, Tradition, Travel, Variety, Wealth, Wisdom.

This list is by no means all encompassing; it is just a starting point. The English language has a lot of different words and we have a lot of different values so another word or value might resonate more for you. Go with that. This is just to give you some ideas and get you started.

Here are some questions to help you identify some of your current values.

- Which of the values mentioned above ring true for you?
- When does it feel okay to spend money?
- Why would you want to save money?
- If you were given $5,000 how would you save, invest or spend it and why? What about $10,000 or $50,000?
- Which of your past financial decisions are your most proud of?
- What about a financial decision you are most ashamed of or was a big mistake and why?
- How do you feel when it's time to make a big financial decision?
- Are you spending money on items or experiences that have meaning to you? Why or why not?
- Do you spend in ways that feel important? What kind of spending would feel important?

- What do you want your life to look like and how could money help?
- How does the best version of yourself, the person you are proud to be, spend, save or invest their money?
- What does financial success look like for you?
- What is the purpose of money in your life?

These are just a few ideas and questions to get the wheels turning. Often we have a lot of these values in varying degrees but we are trying to find the most important ones to prioritize and put our money towards first.

If you are still struggling to determine which values are most important to you, try this little thought experiment. If you were given $500 today, how would you prefer to spend the money between two options?

- If you had the choice between home life and appearance, which would you spend the money on?
- If you had the choice between friends and travel, which would you spend the money on?
- If you had the choice between security and entertainment, which would you spend the money on?

This can help you narrow in on the values that are most important to you.

If you are in an intimate relationship it can be beneficial to have an open conversation about your financial values with your partner or spouse and find out where you may have overlapping values and where you may have different values.

For example, I often find in relationships one spouse will prioritize a value for security and the other will prioritize a value for adventure. Then the question becomes do you save your money for an emergency fund or spend it on a trip? There is no right or wrong answer, but there usually is a way to find a good balance. You can save up to a certain amount to address the desire for security and then set aside a certain amount each year for a trip to address the desire for adventure.

Almost always I find that there will be some overlap in values where both people in the relationship can find common ground, such as a value for connection with friends and family. It can be really helpful to talk about why it is important for each of you to spend or save your money in a certain way. And frankly if you have absolutely no financial values in common - it is going to be a difficult relationship.

Take some time to really sit down and understand each other's values and what the right balance is for your lives. When you create your family's financial values together it is not only great for your relationship, it is also great for your children and creates a positive relationship with money for them as well. It might not be the most comfortable topic at first, but I promise this will help both you and your family in the long run.

Once you have a good idea what some of your personal values are, you can begin setting the right financial goals to match your family's financial priorities.

Grab your journal and answer the following questions:

- What does it appear that you value based on what you are currently spending your money on?
- What has become less of a priority that you want to spend less money on?
- What values do you want to prioritize and put your money towards going forward?

Now take a look at the list of values that you have come up with and circle the 5 most important. The 5 that feel as though they ring true for you. Go ahead and prioritize them by listing them 1-5 so you know what you are going to focus on first.

HOW CAN YOU SAVE AND SPEND IN ALIGNMENT?

Now that we've touched on what your personal values are, let's talk about what it really means to be in alignment with these values.

Shopping and spending can be so fun! You buy that gorgeous new dress you saw in the window, the latest and greatest iPhone that just came out, or that new gadget that caught your eye on Amazon. You get a rush carrying all those new bags home or opening your new presents when the Amazon box arrives! But then later find yourself feeling a little guilty thinking, "Ahh I spent too much money. Why did I buy it? Why do I keep doing this? I didn't really need that." Sometimes you return the items, but more often than not you don't and you just feel guilty as it happens over and over again.

If you are feeling a sense of guilt it may mean that your current spending is not in alignment with your goals and values. If that's the case, don't worry, it's okay, most people are out of alignment at some point in their life. I know I've been there before as I kept trying to "keep up with the Jones'" but guess what? My values looked very different from the Jones,' which is why I was so unhappy and felt guilty. When you spend in alignment with YOUR values and not theirs the guilt and discomfort disappears and is replaced with happiness, pride, and peace.

Perhaps after looking at your current spending you realize you have been prioritizing your value for entertainment. However, it just doesn't sit right because right now home life has become a higher priority in your life. Then it's time to shift your spending towards home life.

Or perhaps after looking at your current spending you find out you are prioritizing your value for security and you are still putting a lot towards this category, but you've actually noticed that relationships have become a higher priority in your life. That's okay. It's time to shift your spending away from security and towards your relationships.

It is an ongoing process because our values can and do change over time.

The key is to align our savings and spending with our goals and current values now to truly feel at peace with our finances. There are lots of stories you hear about where there is a millionaire who you think should be happy but is just miserable. Does Ebenezer Scrooge from *A Christmas Carol* ring a bell? I mean my goodness these millionaires have millions and millions of dollars, how can they not be happy?

It is because of this simple fact...money WILL NOT make you happy.

It is what you DO with your money that can bring you peace and joy. And what you do with your money is based on what your goals and your values are. When you are not using your money in alignment with these goals and values it will not bring you joy.

You may not have everything look exactly as you'd like with your financial picture, but I promise that once you start saving and spending in alignment with your goals and values you will start feeling so much better.

Just that feeling of knowing you are in alignment will change your brain chemistry, change your focus, and will immediately improve your chances of financial success.

Part of what we are talking about here is our relationship with money. It is one of the most important relationships in our life and it is barely talked about in school or with our families growing up. Yet, it has no doubt affected your life and brought you to where you are today. I mean think about it, your relationship with money is something you will have throughout your whole life.

People may come and go but your relationship with money will always be there. This relationship develops whether you realize it or not, so it's probably a good idea to make sure your relationship with money is a healthy one. The surprising thing is how little we talk about money and finance as we grow up and how volatile this relationship with money can be for so many people. I can assure you that your relationship with money is an important relationship for you to foster and support.

You deserve a good, healthy relationship with your money that will make you happy, support you, and help you become a better person. Let's ensure you have a positive relationship with money and are using it to act in alignment with your goals and values. Also, a positive relationship with money doesn't mean you should save all your money, you should spend it too. You will have a healthy relationship with money when you spend and save in alignment with your values and your goals.

At the end of the day, you know you are going to spend money. I'm not saying don't spend money ever and save every penny you ever make. What I am saying is why not spend your money on the things you value that will support your overarching goals?

For example, let's say one of your top 5 values is style. You went to school for interior design and you absolutely love following the latest fashions and you meet your clients in person and your fashion, style, and appearance is very important to you. Then BY ALL MEANS buy yourself those fabulous new Jimmy Choo shoes that you are going to love and wear every single day! Just make sure you balance it out by spending less on things that you don't really value. Like if you are paying several hundred dollars a month on your cable TV when it really doesn't matter that much to you. You are almost never at home to watch TV and when you are you only watch Netflix anyway. Then cut out the cable TV. It is not serving you. It doesn't align with your values and it doesn't support your goals.

Find the right trade offs that align with your values. And yes, I know that sometimes we have other people's values that we are trying to balance between as well. I can hear you saying, "Well yeah maybe I don't value cable TV, but it is a high value for my spouse because he loves being able to watch the sports channels." That's okay, just find out what the right balance is for you all. In our house we only pay for cable during football season and my fiancé is happy because he gets to watch his games and I am happy because we are not spending money on it when we don't use it.

Okay, so one of my core values is for security which I've noticed is common for a lot of the ladies I know. It is very important for me to feel safe and secure. I'm scared of not having enough money for me and my family if something bad were to happen.

You know...apocalypse, alien invasion, world war III, zombies, not having enough money to live on when I'm old, or not being able to eat at my favorite Mexican restaurant.. Very, very bad.

But in all seriousness this need for safety and security is real for me. That's why it's important to me to have enough money to ensure me and my family are secure. In real terms that amounts to me having a healthy emergency fund, a life insurance policy, a strong retirement account, and to build passive income strategies to ensure we can support ourselves in old age.

Working towards these goals and having money for these things makes me feel more secure, which, in turn, makes me happier and I feel aligned with how I am spending my money. If I spent all my money on random stuff every month and didn't have an emergency fund saved up, I would feel the opposite of secure. I'd feel anxious and scared and would not be living in alignment with my core value of security.

Another core value I have is for education. When I spend my money in alignment with that core value it feels good. I love buying books that teach me something new. (I also love fantasy and fiction books that are fun to read too. I am a very avid reader!) However, if I took that same $20 that I spent on a book and bought another new tank top I would most likely regret it and feel a little guilty afterwards thinking to myself…"Well I didn't really need a new tank top. It is nice, but I already have several others like it that are just fine and this purchase doesn't bring me any closer to my goals." Now there is absolutely nothing wrong with buying a new tank top if you really need a new tank top. It's just that for my core values and my current goals it is not high up on my list of priorities.

Along with education I also value personal growth and so I feel good about spending my money on new courses or workshops that teach me something new and help me grow. Some of these workshops are really expensive! To help me determine if I am making the right decision or if I would be better off putting that money towards something else I just think about whether or not the purchase is in alignment with my values and my current goals. Would the knowledge I'd learn help me accomplish my current goals or grow to become the person I want to be? Is there a clear return of investment (ROI) if I purchase this? If so, then I can move forward happily and purchase it. If it's teaching something that doesn't really align with what I currently need for my goals, I can confidently say no it's not for me.

The trouble is marketing and advertising is in our faces every single day and is meant to lure us into spending our money on countless different things.

"Look at this gorgeous tank top, it is the most beautiful tank top this season, it is the perfect shade of magenta and you will look stunning in it."

IT IS CONSTANT. We are constantly inundated with advertising everywhere for everything you could possibly imagine. It is up to us to determine whether those purchases are in alignment and make sense for us or not. Some would and some wouldn't. Completely depends on the person, their values, their goals, and their priorities.

Marketing and advertising is just trying to fill a need or want that we have and that's okay. Their job is to get their product out in front of lots of eyes for people to buy. The trouble is when we haven't decided what we really need or want ahead of time. Then our money is pulled in all these other directions instead of where we actually want it to go. We need to decide where it should go based on our personal priorities and then spend and save accordingly. It is all about the right balance.

Do your financial goals match with your current values and priorities? Yes or no.

Does your spending align and help you achieve your financial goals? Yes or no.

Every time you go to make a purchase just ask yourself, "Does this align with my current values and current goals?" Yes or no.

Let's say your core values are family, travel, health, loyalty, and education and you were contemplating taking a trip to Europe. As someone who values travel and adventure and new experiences a trip aligns completely with your core value for travel. However, what if your best friend's wedding was the exact same weekend, what then? Well you also value loyalty and if your core value of loyalty to your friends and family is stronger than your value for travel and adventure you would probably stay for your friend's wedding and skip the trip.

If there were no conflicting values for the trip though you would probably take the trip. What if the trip actually aligns with several of your core values. You would all go as a family (family value) and there will be walking and hiking during the trip (health value) and you will learn a new language while you are there (education value). Then for this person the purchase of this trip really strongly aligns with their values and they will be very happy saving up their money to spend on this trip! Afterwards they will probably say, "Money well spent!"

Let's say we have a different person whose core values are home life, security, relationships, freedom, and achievement who is contemplating the same trip to Europe. As someone who values freedom this could potentially align with one of their core values. However, what if their value for security or home life is stronger? Then they will want to ensure they are financially secure before they consider a trip like this. They may also want to save up for a new house before spending on a trip like this. So, their first priority will be to build up an emergency fund, then second priority is to save for a down payment. Only once those goals are accomplished would they consider spending their money to go on the trip to Europe.

There is no right or wrong when it comes to this. It just depends on what you value the most, your goals, and where your priorities are. Most likely not all of your core values have the exact same weight and you should think through which ones take first priority and set your financial goals accordingly. Once you have those identified, then you can ensure you spend your money in alignment and you will feel so much better and happier with your money in the process.

WHAT DO YOU WANT?

Let's take this one step further and really dive into what you want by setting your financial goals.

> "Goal setting literally alters the structure of your brain so that you perceive and behave in ways that will cause you to achieve those goals...Challenging goals that have strong emotional resonance will alter your brain structure more quickly and effectively than weak goals." - Geoffrey James

---

James explains in his article, "What Goal-Setting Does to Your Brain and Why It's Spectacularly Effective," that your brain has something called neuroplasticity and when you connect your emotions to a goal you can LITERALLY change the structure of your brain so that it is optimized to achieve that goal.

Wow, I think that is so cool! We actually have the power to change what our brain will focus on by creating really clear and emotionally charged goals, which will make us more likely to accomplish them.

What are your financial goals? How do we ensure

that we set really clear, specific and emotionally charged goals for you?

A financial goal is just something you want to achieve with your money over a specific period of time. It could be building an emergency fund, becoming debt free, going on an incredible vacation, saving up for a down payment to buy a house, or buying that stunning guitar you've always wanted. Keep in mind your goals don't have to be tied to purchases, it can be anything you want to achieve with your money.

Whatever your goal is, let's ensure that it is a very specific, clear goal.

I know you all have probably heard of SMART goals before and, if you're like me, you are a little bit sick of hearing about SMART goals - specific, measurable, attainable, realistic, and time based. Or is it specific, measurable, achievable, relevant and timely? Or how about specific, measurable, actionable, realistic, and time bound? I've seen it referenced so many different ways and feel like every financial article I read talks about SMART goals of some sort.

However, I have done a lot of goal setting in my life and personally have found that SMART goals are missing a few pieces of the puzzle. The emotion connected to your goal for one and the actual plan for how you will achieve your goal for another. A SMART goal is a good start but there is a better way, and since this is my book, we will do things my way!

My favorite way to set a goal (whether financial or not)

is with the 7 questions: Who, What, Where, When, Why, How Much, and How?

If you can answer each of these questions for your goal, then you will have a very clear, specific, and emotionally charged goal with a plan to achieve it.

1. Who - who is involved in achieving this goal?
2. What - what are you trying to achieve?
3. Where - where will your money be saved, invested, or spent?
4. When - by when will you accomplish this goal?
5. Why - why is it important to achieve this goal?
6. How much - how much money is involved?
7. How - how will you actually accomplish this goal?

Now let's go a little bit deeper into each of these questions and then look at an example.

Who - who is involved in accomplishing this goal? I'll make this easy on you, the answer is YOU! You are always the person who is responsible for your life, your goals, and your success. Although sometimes there are other people related to the accomplishment of your goal as well, so it is helpful to identify those people up front.

For example, if you are married, your spouse's spending and saving behaviors will, in all likelihood, affect your goal. If you have a goal to earn more money, then either your current employer or a new employer is a key player for you to accomplish your goal. Take a minute to identify the who for your goal. Remember YOU are still always the most important "who" in order to accomplish your goal.

What - what is your actual goal, what are you trying to achieve, what do you want? Here are a few examples of different financial goals either I've had or my friends and family have had for you to consider:

- Save up an emergency fund
- Pay off all credit card debt
- Take my family on our dream vacation
- Have a positive net worth
- Create a Christmas gift fund
- Earn more money from my job
- Improve my credit score
- Save a down payment for a house
- Renovate my home
- Decorate my home
- Pay off all student loan debt
- Invest in the stock market
- Invest in cryptocurrencies
- Invest in real estate
- Buy an engagement ring
- Save up for our dream wedding
- Create positive cash flow every month
- Get life insurance
- Buy my car in cash completely debt-free
- Earn money from a side hustle
- Save for a child's college education

- Save for retirement
- Have $1MM net worth before I turn 40 years old
- Become completely debt-free
- Save up money to start a business
- Buy a vacation home
- Pay off my mortgage
- Give money every month to a worthy cause

Where - where will your money actually be saved, invested, spent or given? Often with our financial goals we are trying to save towards something, invest in something, or pay off a debt. It is very helpful to take a few minutes to decide where you will actually save, invest, or spend your money. This really helps with the practical planning aspect of your goal. For example, if you are saving for a down payment for a house, where will your money be saved or invested while you build up this down payment? A savings account, an investment account, a checking account, a cryptocurrency account, under your mattress? Where will this money be so you can keep track of your progress? Where do you look to see if you are getting closer to achieving your goal? A financial management app, a loan payment system, a financial statement? Just take a minute to think about it and it's okay if you aren't sure right away. Also if you are new to investing I have a few suggestions on where you can invest your money in chapter 6.

When - by when will you accomplish your goal? What

is the timeline? Is it within a month, a year, several years? It is important to set a specific timeline for your goal in order to be able to track your progress. This helps you measure your progress and see if you are on track with your timeline, ahead of schedule, or behind schedule. We can have both short term and long term financial goals. The important thing is to just set a timeline for when you will accomplish your goal by.

Why - why do you want to achieve this goal? What is the emotional connection that will really drive you to accomplish your goal? Is it for your children? Is it to stop feeling pain, fear, anxiety? Is it to start feeling joy, love, connection?

This is the most often overlooked aspect of goal setting that is crucial to success. You have to discover your why. Why is this important to you? Once you are able to do that and really feel the emotions for why it is important for you to improve your finances or accomplish your goal then I know you will succeed.

If you are struggling to determine your why, my favorite exercise to really dive deep into my why is with the 7 whys exercise that I first learned from Dean Graziosi. It is a simple exercise where you ask yourself why 7 times going a little bit deeper each time.

Here is an example of when I've done this exercise in the past.

1. Why do you want to improve your financial picture? Because I want to have more money

2. Why do you want more money? Because I want to have enough money to cover my expenses every month
3. Why do you want to have enough money to cover your expenses? Because I do not want to have to feel stuck in my full-time job anymore
4. Why do you want to not have a full-time job anymore? Because I don't want to have to wait until I retire to spend my time how I want
5. Why do you want to spend your time how you want right now? Because I want to take time for vacations and important holidays without having to ask for permission and have time freedom while I'm still young
6. Why do you want time freedom while you are still young? Because I want to be able to spend time with my family and friends whenever I want
7. Why do you want the freedom to spend time with your family and friends? Because what is most important to me are the people in my life - my fiancé, my family, my friends and my time with them is the most valuable thing to me right now

Keep in mind you can also do this with 5 whys or 11 whys, the important thing is to just keep asking why until you FEEL something. Until you find the real emotional reason that is driving you that will keep you motivated when it gets challenging.

How much - how much do you need to accomplish your goal? Keeping in mind the timeline you outlined earlier, you can determine exactly how much money you need to accomplish your goal. This is the other component that is so important to be able to measure whether you are on track with your goal. Is it $1,000, $10,000, or $100,000? Just make sure you determine the actual dollar amount it will take for you to accomplish your goal.

If your goal is related to saving a portion of your income, a good rule of thumb is to keep anywhere from 10-20% of your income for yourself to put towards your goals. The more you keep for yourself now, the better off you will be in the future.

How - how will you accomplish your goal? What is your plan? What do you need to do in order to actually accomplish this goal?

I've saved the "how" for last because this is where you create your detailed plan. I will help you come up with an even more specific "how" in the next 2 chapters. Your plan is crucial to help you see that your goal is achievable, to know exactly what you need to do to make it happen, and to help you succeed. If you take a little time up front to come up with your plan, then you are so much more likely to succeed.

Most often the "how" of our financial goals includes increasing your positive cash flow so you have more money to put towards your goal. You can increase your cash flow in one of two ways:

- Earn more
- Spend less

Your "how" is usually just the plan for how to earn more and spend less and then save and invest the positive cash flow this creates.

Here is an example of how to use the 7 questions to set your financial goal.

1. Who - me and my fiancé.
2. What - save for a downpayment for a house.
3. Where - investment account with Betterment.
4. When - 5 years from today August 31, 2026.
5. Why - for a place to call our own where our children can grow up in a safe neighborhood with good schools.
6. How much - $30,000 for down payment. $30,000/5 years = $6,000 a year. $6,000/12 months = $500 a month.
7. How - positive cash flow every month of $500 to automatically transfer into our Betterment investment account. To achieve positive cash flow we will need to earn $300 extra a month from our small business, and spend $200 less on eating out at restaurants, Amazon purchases, and Target purchases. We will transfer $500

directly into our investment account 2 days after our paycheck is deposited into our account before we spend it.

I recommend checking in on your financial goals every month at the same time you prepare your monthly financial statements. Let's get into the habit of setting and measuring these goals consistently every month regardless of whether the timeline for the goal is short (under 1 year) or long (over 1 year). By checking in every month it gives you a chance to see how you are progressing, see if you are on track with your goal, or if you need to make any changes in your lifestyle or your goal.

WHAT'S THE #1 FINANCIAL GOAL EVERYONE SHOULD START WITH?

I know our financial goals will look a little different for each of us. However, there really is one financial goal we should all start with for our financial security and that is an emergency fund. This can be called many things: a rainy day fund, savings account, emergency fund, or reserve account, but it is really all the same thing! It is all in reference to creating a financial buffer for yourself to cover unexpected expenses.

In order to create an emergency fund or a financial buffer for yourself you must have positive cash flow. So, as soon as we begin creating positive cash flow by following our *Saving & Spending Plan*, which is covered in the next chapter, this is the first financial goal I always encourage my friends to focus on.

For example, have you ever been surprised with any of the following:

- Job loss (hello COVID-19...remember that)
- Medical emergency
- Car repair
- Long term care for a parent or loved one
- House repair
- Pet emergency
- Funeral expenses
- Required travel expenses
- School expenses

I know I certainly have. Just the other day my 2005 Mini Cooper S started screeching every time I turned the wheel all the way to the left or to the right. That definitely did not sound good, so I took it into the shop for a few hundred dollars worth of repair. When it really comes down to it, unexpected things happen. When these unexpected things are fun and pleasant we call them a surprise; when they are not fun we usually call them emergencies.

I can't predict the future, if you can...please give me a call...let's talk stocks. However, I do know that unexpected things occur every single year. Although I don't know what the unexpected thing for that year will be, I know that something unexpected will happen EVERY SINGLE

YEAR. It just happens, so let's empower you to be ready for when it does.

I've been asked over and over again, "Okay but how much should I put aside in an emergency fund?"

I'll give everyone's least favorite answer first. It depends. It really does depend on your financial situation. However, I also have a slightly more satisfying answer as well.

If you need a rule of thumb, put aside AT LEAST 3 months worth of expenses into your emergency account. After completing your *Income & Expense Statement,* if you have on average $3,500 in expenses every month, then start with a $10,500 emergency fund ($3,500*3 months).

If you aren't quite sure yet how much your expenses are each month but still need a number to start with then set a goal for a $20,000 emergency fund.

Here are a few other questions to consider when deciding whether to increase or decrease your emergency fund amount:

How reliable is your income source?

- The more reliable the income from your job is, the less you need to set aside in case you were to lose your job. Keep in mind though, no matter what your company has said to you, in their mind you are replaceable, even if they really like you - harsh but true. Examples - great depression, housing bubble, COVID-19...it happens.

How long would it take you to find a new income source?

- If you know it has taken you 6 months in the past to find a new job because of your specific skill set then you need to set aside enough in an emergency fund to cover at least 6 months of expenses.

Does your income fluctuate each month?

- Is it a fixed paycheck amount every month or does it fluctuate based on commission or other seasonal factors? If it tends to fluctuate each month then you need to set aside more to give yourself a buffer on the lower income months.

Do you have large expenses that may be coming up soon?

- Is your car on its last leg and you may have to buy a new one soon? Has someone in your family been having a lot of medical problems recently? Is your computer making that weird sound every time you log on and needs to be replaced? If you have large expenses you think will be coming up soon then set aside a little extra in your emergency fund.

These are just a few things to consider when deciding on your emergency fund amount. Remember, something is better than nothing and more is better than something.

The crazy thing I've found with emergency funds is that once you have one set up, you have less emergencies, and when you don't have one, emergencies will keep popping up until you set one aside. I think it's one of those funny little pranks the universe likes to play with us to teach us a lesson. So, please just take my advice and set one up or at least tell me your crazy story when the universe decides to play!

MONEY MOVERS

- Identify and write down your top 5 financial values. Prioritize them by ranking them 1-5.
- Write down your top 1 or 2 financial goals based on your current values. Be very specific with your goals by asking the 7 questions: who, what, where, when, why, how much, and how?

SAVING & SPENDING PLAN

"Money is only a tool. It will take you wherever you wish, but it will not replace you as the driver." - Ayn Rand

Now it's time to get into the nitty gritty and create a plan. Remember in the last chapter when you were setting your goal there were 7 questions to ask: who, what, where, when, why, how much, and how.

Okay, good. We are about to dive in deeper on the "how." Regardless of your specific financial goal, almost all of them are related to this question, "How do I actually increase my income and/or lower my expenses to generate the positive cash flow needed to accomplish my goal?"

WHAT IS MY *SAVING & SPENDING PLAN*?

For that you need a *Saving and Spending Plan* more commonly known as a BUDGET...dun...dun...dun. I know a budget, ugh, not my favorite word, but all it really comes down to is your plan to save and spend your money the way you want to. With intention, purposefully.

I'd really like to take the fear out of this word "budget" if I can. When I hear the word budget my thoughts immediately go to, "I'm going to have to live off rice and beans and won't be allowed to spend any money on anything fun and it's going to be miserable. Ugh. I don't want to have a budget."

If you have a similar reaction, I don't blame you and am not surprised. The reason I think we have that reaction is because so often we are trying to create the strategy for our money and finances before we have addressed our values and goals.

Remember how I said that the order needs to be:

1. Understand your values
2. Set your goals
3. Determine your strategy

Well, the budget is just your strategy but if you haven't really understood your values and goals then all it feels like is a bunch of rules you have to follow with your money that is no fun.

When you really start to understand your values and

goals, then creating a budget is just a plan to help us align with our values and accomplish our goals, which are the things we want! Notice I said saving AND spending. You can still spend your money on things you want.

Do you have to prioritize your spending and make some sacrifices? Yes, but if you really want to accomplish your goal, you'll have the reason and motivation behind you. You will see this as a step towards what you really want in the long-term, not just a reaction to everything around you in the short-term. That's why I said it is so important when setting your goal to dive deep into the reason why you want to accomplish your goal. The "why" is what will keep you committed and moving forward.

However, what you want to prioritize and what you want to sacrifice is 100% completely up to you! I am not going to decide that for you. If you are like, "You know what Jess, I absolutely love love love going to concerts. I really strongly value music in my life and I am 100% happy putting my money towards supporting my favorite musicians!"

Amazing, I love it, you DO NOT have to give that up. I will repeat, you DO NOT have to give up everything you love to spend your money on. However, you DO need to create positive cash flow at the end of each month so you need to answer the question, "What is something you don't value as much that you can cut back on in the meantime?"

Maybe you keep your concerts but spend less on things for your house Or you keep your concerts but spend less on ordering delivery or eating out because those aren't as high up on your list of priorities and values.

Also, keep in mind, this is not a forever decision. This is a short term decision to get your spending and saving in line to help you accomplish what you want in the long term. You will not have to live by it forever.

In fact, the crazy thing is once I see my friends put in place their new *Saving and Spending Plan,* they are usually able to accomplish their goals so much quicker than they really thought they could!

For example, let's say your goal is to be completely free of your student loan debt once and for all. This feels like a huge monster of a task that will take forever, so we are hesitant to sacrifice anything for it. It seems like we will have to do without for such a long time, but once you get rolling with some momentum, I almost always see my friends accomplish their goals early. Often I hear, "That wasn't as bad as I thought it would be." Once you start improving your financial picture and putting all the right habits and strategies in place it just gets better and better and better.

To create a *Saving & Spending Plan* all we have to do is take the layout of your *Income & Expense Statement* and turn it into a plan for what you want to do with your income and your expenses next month. How do you want to spend and save your money? That is your *Saving & Spending Plan.*

Your *Income & Expense Statement* reflects what actually

happened with your income and expenses over the past month.

Income & Expense Statement = actual cash flow from the past

Your *Saving & Spending Plan* (aka your budget) is your plan for what you want to do with your income and expenses for a future month.

Saving & Spending Plan = plan for future cash flow

There are two components that come into play for your *Saving and Spending Plan*. Can you guess what they are? Hint, hint … we addressed them in chapter 2. Yup, that's right. Income and expenses.

As we mentioned earlier, the formula for cash flow is:

Income - Expenses = Cash Flow

In order to have positive cash flow we need our income to be greater than our expenses. There are two ways we can do this:

1. Increase our income
2. Decrease our expenses

90% of financial articles on the internet focus on #2 and how to decrease your expenses, but I think it is equally important to bring your attention to #1 and how to increase your income as well. You will always be limited with how much positive cash flow you can create by only focusing on how to decrease your expenses. However, if you focus on how to increase your income as well, your positive cash flow options become much broader.

If you want to expedite your path to financial freedom, you would be wise to both increase your income and decrease your expenses simultaneously. Let's take a look at how we can do both of these things.

HOW CAN I INCREASE MY INCOME?

One way to improve your month end cash flow is to increase the income side of the equation. Simply put, if you earn more, then you have more wiggle room to create positive cash flow. So, how can we earn more?

There are lots of different ways by tapping into one or more of the 7 different income sources. Here are 7 different active and passive income sources:

1. Earned Income
2. Business Income
3. Interest Income
4. Dividend Income
5. Rental Income
6. Capital Gains Income
7. Royalty Income

Please note there are both active and passive income sources on this list. With active income sources you are actively trading your time for money. This is where you do some work or provide a service and someone pays you for it. If you do not actively continue working, you will not receive any income.

For example, if you are a dog walker you trade the service of walking dogs for income. If you continue to book dog walking appointments and walk dogs you will continue to earn income. When you stop walking dogs your income stops.

Whereas, other sources of income are considered passive and you do not actively trade your time for money. Passive income is where your income is not directly tied to the time you spend working. Please do not misunderstand me, there is still work involved. The difference is the work for a passive income stream usually takes place early on, then once the product or service you worked on is established the income continues to flow later. It is not directly related to your time. You could stop actively working on the product but continue to receive income.

For example, if you invest in a stock you put in work up front to research the company and understand their business and profitability. Once you have invested in the stock of the company, so long as it is profitable, it will continue to pay you dividends every month without any additional effort or work required on your part. As long as the business continues to do well, your income will continue.

In general, the 7 income sources fall into these categories:

- Earned Income - active
- Business Income - active or passive depending on the business
- Interest Income - passive
- Dividend Income - passive
- Rental Income - active or passive depending on property management
- Capital Gains Income - passive
- Royalty Income - passive

Earned Income - The first is the most well known and most common income source. Earned income is what you make from a job that you have been hired to do. Most people start here and many go no further. This is an active income source where you are often required to trade your time for money and as soon as you stop producing, your income will also stop. You can always increase the income side of the equation by getting another full-time or part-time job that provides earned income. It is often called a side hustle when you get another job on the side to quickly increase your income. You can also strive to increase your earned income through a promotion or job change. Although this is a good starting point, I highly encourage you to explore some of the other more passive income sources.

Business Income - This is the profit or income you create with positive cash flow from a business. You can become an entrepreneur and start your own business selling a product or service to generate additional business income or profit. Just remember this only helps if you are truly able to generate positive cash flow. A business operating at a loss will magnify your personal finance problems, not help them. There are risks involved with this path and income source, but when done right I have found it to ultimately be a very rewarding path to take.

Interest Income - This is one of the best passive income streams available and the ones that banks and financial institutions use to generate significant profits for their businesses. I highly recommend turning this into an income stream that works in your favor instead of paying it out to others as an expense. You earn interest when you lend your money such as with a bond or Certificate of Deposit or when you put your money into an interest-bearing bank account such as a savings account. You can even earn interest on certain cryptocurrencies now. With this income source you can take advantage of compound interest which is a beautiful thing when it is working in your favor.

Dividend Income - This is another great passive income stream available to you. When you buy shares in a company, such as a stock, you become a part owner or investor in that company and are entitled to dividend payments. Dividend payments are when a company distributes it's taxable income to it's investors. Investing in the right companies in the stock market can generate consistent dividend payments to enhance your income.

Rental Income - Rental income is earned when you own property and rent it out to someone else. This is most often seen with real estate although it can now be seen with cars and bikes and other property as well. Anything that you own that you let someone else rent from you will generate rental income. This can be a great passive income source as well, although there are a few caveats. In order to earn the rental income especially on a real estate property it will require a substantial investment initially to purchase the property. Also if operated as a business, such as doing the property management yourself on a real estate property, this may become more of an active income source. However, when you can step away from the property and just have it rent out every month without too much involvement, it becomes a great passive income source.

Capital Gains Income - Selling an asset that you own for more than what you purchased it for generates income known as capital gains. For example, if you buy a stock for $20 and you sell it for $80, there is a profit of $60 ($80 - $20) which is known as your capital gain. If you buy a real estate property for $300,000 and you sell it for $450,000, then there is a capital gain of $150,000 ($450,000 - $300,000). Keep in mind these capital gains will be taxed either as a short-term capital gain or as a long-term capital gain, which will decrease your capital gains income by the amount of the tax. This is another great passive income source and with a diversified portfolio usually all you need is time to realize your capital gains.

Royalty Income - Last but not least is royalty income, which is another great income source. Royalty income is created by generating, designing, or producing something unique and then charging businesses and/or people to use it. The music industry is a great example of this. When a musician produces a new record they receive royalty payments for each record sold from their record company. This shows how the work for this passive income stream takes place early on when creating the record and then once the record is completed the income continues to flow without any additional work on the musicians part. Also, YouTubers will receive royalty payments when they monetize their videos by showing ads. They will continue to receive royalty payments as long as their videos are generating revenue from their advertising.

Remember, our goal is to increase the income side of the equation in order to increase our positive cash flow every month and there are lots of ways to do this. Especially with technology and the accessibility we have to so many resources online now. The barrier to entry to create a small business for additional business income is lower than it has ever been before in history. Technology has also made it easier than ever to access interest, dividend, and capital gains income sources.

If you put in a little time, thought, and effort I know you can come up with 1 or 2 new ways that you could begin to bring additional income into your life!

HOW CAN I DECREASE MY EXPENSES?

Okay, now for the expense side of the equation. The one that all the financial articles talk about when they talk about a budget.

How do we lower our expenses so that we can create positive cash flow?

That depends. What do you currently spend your money on? With a better understanding of your values and goals where can you cut back? This is a question that every person needs to answer for themselves. I don't know exactly what you value and what your goals are so I don't have a blanket answer that will apply for everyone across the board.

However, I can give you a few ideas for how to figure this out for yourself. Remember when we put together our *Income & Expense Statement* and came up with categories for each of our expenses for the previous month. Now is the time to dig a little deeper into those categories and expenses. I'm sure that when you go through them there will be a few that surprise you or stand out!

Go through the last 3 months and look at all of your expenses. Determine which expenses are fixed, or are the same dollar amount every month, and which expenses are variable, or differ in dollar amount every month.

Fixed expenses will have the same payment amount every month. Take a close look at these fixed expenses first. These could include payments for your:

- Mortgage/Rent
- Car loan
- Student loan
- Credit card loan
- Insurance
- Phone service
- Internet service
- Subscriptions

There is a lot of potential to reduce your expenses in these categories. Remember, just because they are a fixed payment with the same amount each month does not mean you couldn't reduce or eliminate them.

For example:

- You could lower your rent payment if you move to a new apartment with a lower rent or you could add a roommate if you own your own place.
- You could sell that car, pay off the car loan, and buy a car that you can afford with cash or with a lower payment.
- You could lower your cell phone plan or

internet service with a little research into other providers or other less expensive plans.
- You could eliminate any subscriptions that you signed up for that may no longer match your values and goals.

Variable expenses are the ones that cost different amounts every month. Categories for these expenses include:

- Food & Groceries
- Utilities
- Transportation
- Entertainment
- Eating out
- Self care
- Health
- Personal development
- Clothing
- Child care
- Pets
- House
- Travel
- Gifts
- Donations
- Other

You have a lot of different options to reduce these variable expenses as well. For example, you could:

- Lower your grocery bill each month by switching to more price friendly options for a while, such as less steak dinners and more pasta dinners because pasta costs less than steak. You still need groceries of course but you can figure out ways to spend less on your groceries.
- Lower your entertainment budget by attending one less concert, or buying less alcohol, or purchasing less movies. You don't have to eliminate the category completely but look at your values and goals again and look at the expenses in your entertainment category to see if they align or not. Eliminate the ones that don't align.
- Lower your clothing budget by setting a threshold of just one new purchase for the month. This is another way to not completely eliminate a category but pull back a little bit on the spending in that category and really be conscious of how much you are buying in that category.
- Lower your eating out every month with less DoorDash orders, less Starbucks drive through, less dinners out at restaurants, and replace them with groceries, home-brew coffee, and dinners in. When you purchase the groceries yourself and prepare your own meals it will almost always be less than what you are paying for eating out.

I don't really have to tell you where to cut back on your expenses, you are the best person to figure that out. Once you start going through your own expenses you will see where you can cut back.

Some of it will be easy when you are like, "Oh my gosh, I didn't even realize I'm still paying for that magazine subscription that I never read every month. That's easy, time to cancel it!"

Others will be big surprises when you notice, "$200 a month on Chick-Fil-A! Wow, I am really keeping them in business."

Look at all of your expenses (both fixed and variable) and decide if they are still aligned with your values and goals.

If your Chick-Fil-A habit isn't really aligned with your values or goals, then this is probably an area that you can cut back. In fact, if it is in direct opposition to your values and goals (a health value for instance and a goal to lose weight) then all of a sudden this becomes an easy choice.

No more spending on Chick-Fil-A. Done. Now you will have $200 extra towards your cash flow. Then think about where you can begin to spend that money that does align with one of your goals. Perhaps you could put your positive cash flow towards a gym membership. ;)

Now I know this is a little bit easier said than done because a lot of these purchases have become spending habits and sometimes habits can be challenging to break. That's okay, there are lots of tools and strategies out there to help you break these habits, which we will talk about a little later.

For right now, all I want you to do is go through your expenses for the past 3 months and write down in your journal all the expenses you'd like to lower or eliminate. If it is an expense like a subscription you can cancel or change right now, then please go ahead and do it.

HOW DO I BUILD MY *SAVING AND SPENDING PLAN*?

This is my favorite strategy that actually works and it is simply a plan for your money. I bet there is something at some point that you enjoyed planning. Try and remember that feeling of excitement and anticipation when you were planning for something you were looking forward to in the future. Maybe a special trip, a birthday party, dinner with friends, a wedding, or a celebration for someone you cared about. Okay, do you have something in mind?

Now we are going to do the same thing except with our finances. All we are doing is creating a plan for our money that is in our own best interest that will make our own lives so much better, happier, and less stressful in the future.

To build your personal *Saving & Spending Plan* I want you to start by flipping a few pages back in your journal and taking a look at your *Income & Expense Statement*.

We are going to base our *Saving & Spending Plan* off of

our *Income & Expense Statement* with a few tweaks for what we want our future saving and spending to look like.

Okay now flip to a fresh page and write "*SAVING & SPENDING PLAN*" at the top and underline it. Write down "PROJECTED INCOME" underneath the title at the top of the page, "PROJECTED EXPENSES" in the middle of the page, and "POSITIVE CASH FLOW" at the bottom of the page. It should look similar to this.

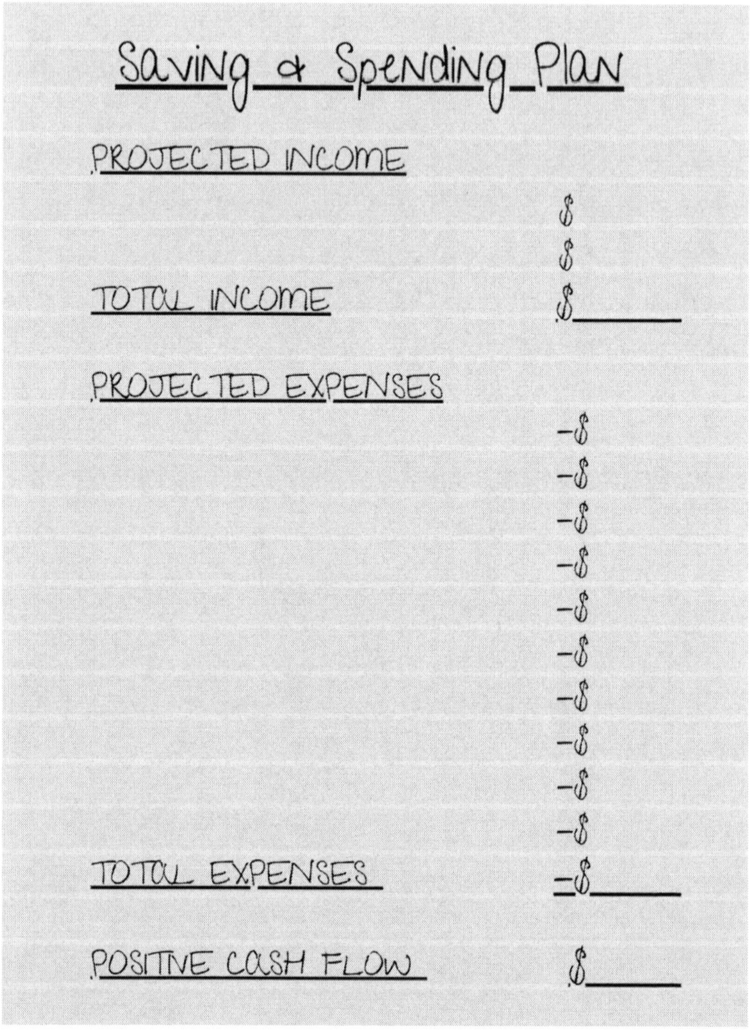
Saving & Spending Plan

PROJECTED INCOME
$
$
TOTAL INCOME $____

PROJECTED EXPENSES
-$
-$
-$
-$
-$
-$
-$
-$
-$
-$
TOTAL EXPENSES -$____

POSITIVE CASH FLOW $____

Now there are 5 steps to creating our *Saving & Spending Plan*:

1. Identify projected income number
2. Identify projected expense number

3. Adjust until positive cash flow number aligns with goal
4. Set up a personal finance app to track expenses
5. Set up an automated transfer to an investment account

Step 1: **Identify projected income** - Let's start with the income, what is your current income? If you have a salaried position, this is usually pretty straight forward. You make the same amount every pay period and can put that number at the top of your saving and spending plan under income.

Let's only include the income that is actually flowing into your checking account or the take-home pay amount you have to cover your bills. Don't worry about your gross income amount before contributions, distributions, and taxes for right now.

Any other consistent income sources, such as child support or Social Security, that you receive every month should be included.

If Grandma gave you $30 for your birthday this month, do not include that. That is a one-time income source, not a consistent income source. Now, if Grandma gives you $200 every single month because you are her favorite, that is a different story. That is consistent income and should be included.

If you have interest and dividend income that is being reinvested in your investment account, do not include that for right now. We are really just looking at consistent income flowing into your checking account.

What if my income varies or is unpredictable?

For my commission based or fluctuating income people I want you to identify one month with your lowest income and one month with your highest income.

You can either:

- Use your lowest income month
- Use an average of your lowest and highest income months

I'd like you to build your saving and spending plan based on your lowest income month amount to be conservative. That way the plan you make for your expenses will not exceed a low income month. Then if you do, in fact, earn more that month it will just be icing on the cake.

Any extra income would increase your positive cash flow for that month and can help you create a buffer in your emergency fund for any future low income months. By being conservative with your spending and aggressive with your saving you will be able to rely on your buffer when you really need it.

If you are like, "Well Jess, that really was way lower and a bit of an outlier," then go ahead and take an average and build your *Saving and Spending Plan* based on your average income month amount instead.

You know your income better than anyone else so just

be as realistic with yourself as you can. If you expect to have a certain level of commission every month include that. If you really aren't sure what you will have coming in for next month, then be a little bit conservative with your income number to give yourself a buffer.

Write down your projected income, total it up, and circle it! Let's say your projected income number is $4,000.

This is going to be the income number for your *Saving & Spending Plan* for right now, but I also want you to start exploring other income sources as well.

On the second page of your *Saving & Spending Plan* write down 1 or 2 of the additional income sources we discussed above and figure out how to start bringing in that additional income as soon as possible.

PROJECTED INCOME

Start a side gig selling on Etsy
Drive for Uber on weekends
Research and invest in cryptocurrency
Invest in a real estate property

Step 2: **Identify projected expenses** - Okay, on to the second slightly trickier step when creating your *Saving & Spending Plan* and that is reviewing your expenses.

Under the expenses section of your *Saving & Spending Plan* I want you to identify any expenses you can eliminate right now. Write them down. Then eliminate them. That means actually cancel the subscriptions right now. If you are getting charged late fees, set up automatic payments right now, so this will not happen in the future. Ready, set go! I will be here waiting....(insert Jeopardy song here!)

Ok, great! Now identify some fixed and variable expense categories that you know you can reduce. Write them down. How are you planning on reducing them? What do you need to do right now to keep yourself from overspending in that category?

Are your expenses less than the income number we circled above?

If not, then you need to keep going through your expenses until this plan reflects a positive cash flow number.

If you've eliminated everything you can think of

except for your basic needs and you still are not showing a positive cash flow number then you must create an additional income source right now (most likely through part-time or full-time earned income.)

Step 3: Adjust until positive cash flow number aligns with goal - Keep refining this plan until you have a positive cash flow number that matches with the financial goal you wrote down earlier. So, if your highest priority financial goal requires $500 a month, keep working on your *Saving & Spending Plan* until you get to your goal of $500 a month in positive cash flow.

Take the time to do this right. Create a realistic plan that you can follow. Think about it, in the past how much time have you spent planning a vacation? How much time have you spent planning a party? How much time have you just spent on social media or watching TV? I would bet you've spent at least an hour or two planning other trips, on social media, or watching TV. You owe it to yourself to spend at least that much time planning your money and financial future as well.

So, instead of watching 2 hours of TV tonight, create a detailed *Saving & Spending Plan* that will change your life. Live your life like you are the hero in your own movie. Act as if there is a documentary crew filming your success story to financial freedom. I promise it will be worth it!

Once you have your plan, I want you to write down the total expense number you need to stay under each month to achieve your goal. Circle it. Under that, write down your positive cash flow goal number (Projected

Income - Projected Expenses) and circle this magical number. Stare at it and give it a little smile!

Saving & Spending Plan

PROJECTED INCOME	
Bi-monthly salary	$2,000
Bi-monthly salary	$2,000
TOTAL INCOME	$4,000
PROJECTED EXPENSES	
Mortgage Loan	-$2,000
Utilities	-$200
Transportation	-$150
Insurance	-$200
Student Loans	-$350
Food	-$300
Entertainment	-$50
Self-Care	-$100
Gifts & Donations	-$50
Other	-$100
TOTAL EXPENSES	-$3,500
POSITIVE CASH FLOW	$500

On the second page of your *Saving & Spending Plan* write down all the ways you will begin to cut back your expenses in order to hit your goal. This step is just as important as the first step to really help you think through what behaviors you will change to make this work.

Saving & Spending Plan

PROJECTED INCOME

Start a side gig selling on Etsy
Drive for Uber on weekends
Research and invest in cryptocurrency
Invest in a real estate property

PROJECTED EXPENSES

Switch to Cricket 2GB cell phone plan
Cancel subscriptions I don't use
For groceries, cut back on expensive cheeses, meats, nuts
2 dinners out at restaurants a month
Only order DoorDash once a month
Only 2 drinks at happy hour
Buy 1 new dress a month
Chick-Fil-A only once a month
No concerts for a little while
Cancel cable and Hulu and just use Netflix

Okay, so let's say I've looked at my expenses for the last 3 months and know I want to spend less on Chick-Fil-A each month. Before I buy it again I am aware that I want to be spending less on it so the thought will cross my mind, "Should I really buy this? Does this purchase align with my goals and values?" However, I'll also be thinking, "I'm hungry, I want Chick-Fil-A, it's delicious, and they are so nice to me." So, you need some strategies to help you actually spend less and save more when these moments arise.

Here's the truth. We all have good intentions with our budget but we also underestimate how much we wind up spending in each category every month. We keep overspending and we keep trying to rely on our self-discipline in every single purchasing decision moment which is really hard and not the best approach. Really this comes down to awareness and behavior change.

I'm sure you've heard of creating an individual budget or amount for each category that you'd like to keep your spending under. For example, you say okay Groceries - $300, Entertainment - $100, Clothing - $150, Other - $200 etc.

But here's the thing, it is so challenging to keep track of all of our expenses in EVERY single category, EVERY single time we make a purchase, EVERY single month. I freaking love finance and numbers and I'm such a nerd about this stuff, and yet even I find this challenging. And I'm someone who is really good at this stuff!

It is a lot to track throughout the month and this category budget system is too reliant on my self-discipline, or lack thereof, every time I am making a purchase. I have a job and a family and a lot going on every month which makes this hard to monitor and stay on top of.

Plus, let's say I do succeed in spending less in one category, the clothing category for example, but then spend way too much in another category, like entertainment, which results in negative cash flow for the month. Then I still have not achieved my overall goal for positive cash flow that month.

Instead, I like to focus on the total expense number approach. That means instead of monitoring your spending for each and every expense category every month, I want your focus to be on not spending more than the total expense number every month.

That means if your total expense number is $3,500 and you look at your spending on the 20th of the month and you've already spent $3,200 that month, you know you'll need to cut back on your spending because you only have $300 left to spend on everything for the entire rest of the month.

I like using this total expense number approach the best because it is only one number to keep track of instead of lots of different numbers for each category. Plus, if an unexpected expense does arise, that's okay, just figure out a way to cut back in some of the other categories for the month so that you don't go over your total expense number.

Step 4: Set up a personal finance app to track expenses - The best way I've found to keep track of your spending is by using a financial app. Technology is an amazing thing and there are so many financial apps available now that help you track your cash flow, net worth, spending, and debt! They make your finances so much easier to look at each month. Instead of having to log into every single financial account you have, you can just link them all under one app and quickly check your app every month to see your current account balances.

I know some people are concerned with the safety and security of connecting all their financial accounts to an app. Let me reassure you that a lot of these apps have been around for quite a while at this point and have put in really great security precautions. I've personally been using them for years now and have not had any problems whatsoever with the security of my bank accounts. In fact, a lot of them have 2 factor authentication to provide added security each time you log in.

Apps like Personal Capital, Mint and HoneyDue are really great free options.

My favorite is Personal Capital because I can keep track of my monthly cash flow, my monthly net worth, and my investments all in the same app. I've found this is the best app to give me a snapshot of my financial picture and help me build wealth. You can link all of your credit cards, checking account, savings account, IRAs, 401K, and loans so you can quickly and easily see everything in one place. The only account that doesn't link in for me right now is my cryptocurrency account. However, with all of this other information linked you can track your current net worth the same way you would in your *Net Worth Statement*.

To fill out my *Net Worth Statement* every month all I have to do is log into the app at the end of the month, make sure all my linked accounts are current and then record the balances. This usually takes me under 5 minutes and I will frequently check my net worth multiple times throughout the month. This literally makes tracking your net worth so easy that you can monitor your net worth every day if you want.

Personal Capital also has both a cash flow and budgeting feature which categorizes your income and expenses so you can easily keep track of your actual cash flow for the month as well as your budgeting goals. You can monitor the expenses tab so you will know when you are getting close to that total expenses number we circled in step 3. You can not only use this app to monitor your net worth, but can also track your income and expenses, set a monthly budget, and even monitor your portfolio investments as well. It is by far my favorite.

I highly recommend downloading Personal Capital to quickly and easily monitor your net worth, cash flow, budgeting, and investment portfolio all in one place. And, no, I don't have a sponsorship deal with Personal Capital, I just really like their product. But if you are from Personal Capital and are reading this book, hit me up!

Mint is another quality free app that tracks both your net worth and your spending. It is one of the oldest and best known budgeting apps and is owned by Intuit which is the same company that makes Quickbooks and Turbotax. Mint comes with a whole range of features with the most popular being its budgeting tools. It alerts you when you're over your budget in a particular category and helps track all your bills in one place with reminders for upcoming payments. It also includes a free credit monitoring service which is nice.

For my lovely couples out there, make sure you link all your individual and joint accounts to your financial app, so you can really track everything together in one place. One of my favorites for couples is HoneyDue so that you can ensure you have positive cash flow as a family every month. That way you don't find out at the end of the month that one of you was on track with your credit card spending but the other went over so you didn't hit your positive cash flow goal. This app helps you see everything together and communicate throughout the month to ensure you work together to meet your goals.

Just remember you want to monitor your expenses to ensure they are under the total expense number you set in your *Saving & Spending Plan* in step 3. That way you will have positive cash flow every month. If you notice your expenses starting to creep up well before the end of the month then cut on your spending to stay on track. I check my app every week to see how I'm doing with my spending usually right before I know I'm about to spend money, like before I go to Costco to buy groceries. Then I'll also check it at the end of the month when reviewing my *Saving & Spending Plan*. When you are first starting out, I would recommend checking it every week until you get used to it. You will be shocked at how much money you can spend in one week!

Step 5: Set up an automated transfer to an investment account - I want you to open an investment account right now and set up an automatic transfer from your checking account to the investment account every single month. That's right, we are going to make this happen!

Before you set up the recurring transfers just do me a favor and ensure you have a little bit of a buffer in your checking account first. A buffer of about one month's worth of expenses will keep you covered. So, if on average you spend about $3,500 a month in expenses just keep an extra $3,500 buffer in your checking account at all times to prevent any overdraft fees that could result from a timing mismatch of your automated payments and transfers.

Okay so you now have enough of a buffer in your checking account and are ready to set up your automated transfer. The next question I usually get is, "But how much do I transfer?"

Let's say when you look at your *Saving & Spending Plan* that your income number is $4,000 and your expense number is $3,500 with a positive cash flow goal of $500 every month. You are going to set up an automatic transfer of UP TO $500 every month.

We are going to transfer up to $500 into either your investment account (for your emergency fund), your 401K account (for retirement), your loan accounts (for debt payoff), your investment account (for your other financial goals), or your IRA (for retirement).

And I really would recommend investing your money into those accounts in that order:

1. Investment account - until you hit your goal for your emergency fund
2. 401K account - until you at least match your employer contribution %
3. Loan account - until you pay off your high interest credit cards and expensive debt
4. Investment account - for your other financial goals
5. IRA account - for any additional retirement saving outside of your company sponsored plan

If you are a little nervous about transferring all $500 every month, that's okay. Start with something a little less like $100 or $200 for the first few months to give you some wiggle room until you are comfortable you really do have that positive cash flow to work with.

Just make sure you set up the automatic transfer for something, even if you can only realistically put aside $10 every month. I really just want you to have the system in place to automatically save for you. This is the saving part of the *Saving & Spending Plan*. Plus when this money automatically transfers out of your account every month it makes it a lot less tempting to spend it.

Let's look at a few scenarios with your $500 positive cash flow number to see how you could put it towards your debt payments and financial goals.

- If you don't have an emergency fund yet, you could start out by transferring all $500 straight into your investment account for the emergency fund until you have it built up to a comfortable level.
- If you have your emergency fund set, then you could ensure you are contributing at least the match amount to your 401K. Let's say you only need $200 to match your 401K plan, then increase your contribution amount through your 401K provider. You still have about $300 leftover. You could then automatically transfer the remaining $300 to pay down your outstanding credit card balances.
- Or if you already have your emergency fund covered, are matching your 401K plan, and have paid off all your debt, you can take your $500 and automatically transfer it to your investment account to save up for a down payment on a home or for your next fabulous vacation. You can begin investing that money into whatever your top priority financial goal is.

Also you can always start out with a slightly smaller amount than the full positive cash flow goal amount to get comfortable with the process. The important thing is to just get these transfers in place and set up. So, even if you know you are going to focus on paying down your debt first, you can still set up an investment account with an automatic transfer of $10 every month. Then it will be easy to just change the amount you transfer later as your priorities change.

Set up the automatic transfer to occur 1-2 days after your paycheck hits your checking account. If you receive your paycheck twice a month then you could also set up 2 automatic transfers per month, one after each paycheck.

Have you ever heard anyone say "pay yourself first?" That is essentially what we are doing. We work hard for our money and we deserve to keep some of it and apply it towards our goals. I like to have my money transferred right after my first paycheck comes in, so I'm not tempted to spend it for the rest of the month. With this strategy I don't have to rely on my self-discipline with every single purchase I make or worry about transferring whatever money I have left over at the end of the month to my investment account. It is already done automatically for me and I know every month I am progressing towards my financial goals. Pay yourself first!

Okay, but WHERE do I actually invest this money?

There are so many different investment accounts and providers out there, which I think of in 3 categories.

- Traditional financial advisors and investment accounts

- Do-it-yourself investment accounts
- Robo advisors and investment accounts

With traditional financial advisors you have an experienced advisor with your financial institution manage your investments and you usually pay for it with higher management fees.

With a do-it-yourself investment account approach you manage your investments yourself and you usually have much lower management fees.

However, one of the easiest ways to get started with investing is through robo advisors. I love robo advisors and I recommend them to all my friends. They make it easy to start investing without a lot of financial background and have the goldilocks of investment fees - not too expensive, not too cheap, they are "just right."

Robo advisors are right in between traditional financial advisors and the do-it-yourself investment platforms. They are able to use advanced computer algorithms to ask you questions about your goals, understand your risk tolerance, and invest your money to align with your goals. They make it really straightforward and easy for anyone who is just starting out in the investment world. All you have to do is answer a few questions about yourself and your goals when you create your account.

For instance, they will be asking you questions like:

- What is your goal?
- How much do you plan to invest initially?

- How much do you want to add to your account automatically and how often?
- What is your time horizon?
- What level of risk are you comfortable with?

Once you answer all of their questions, they will run a quick analysis of your situation and, based on your goal and risk tolerance, will recommend where to invest your money in order to achieve your goal in the given time frame.

There are a lot of different robo advisors out there and I encourage you to check them out and find the right one for you.

Right now my favorites are:

- Wealthfront
- Betterment
- Ellevest
- E*Trade

Check them out, pick one, and take a few minutes to set up your investment account and automatic transfers right now!

MONEY MOVERS

- Build out and implement your *Saving & Spending Plan.* Write down your income number and circle it. Write down your expense number and circle it. Write down your positive cash flow number and circle it.

- Identify 1 or 2 new ways you can increase your monthly income.
- Identify 5 to 10 new ways you can decrease your monthly expenses.
- Sign up for one financial app to track your expenses and link your financial accounts.
- Open a new investment account with a robo advisor for your emergency fund and financial goals.
- Set up a monthly automatic transfer to your investment, retirement, or loan accounts of UP TO your positive cash flow number.

DEBT PAYOFF PLAN

"To achieve what 1% of the world's population has (financial freedom), you must be willing to do what only 1% dare to do...hard work and perseverance of the highest order." - Manoj Arora

Debt keeps you stuck, unable to build wealth, delays your financial goals, robs your present, and steals from your future. There are all sorts of reasons people choose to remain stuck in debt instead of taking the right steps to become debt free, but don't let these reasons hold you back any longer.

Here are some of the most common reasons I've seen why people stay in debt:

- They're trying to keep up with the Jones' or keep up appearances

- They're unwilling to make short term sacrifices for long term gains
- They don't make it a priority
- They don't have a well thought out plan
- They think it's someone else's fault

Does one of these reasons ring true for you? I understand if they do and I also know that it is time to let some of those reasons go so you can move forward.

> "Getting over a painful experience is much like crossing the monkey bars. You have to let go at some point in order to move forward." - C.S. Lewis

---

On the flip side, I've also seen and heard lots of reasons people choose to get out of debt. Here are just a few inspiring stories of people who have made it out of debt from the *NerdWallet* article, "How They Ditched Debt."

> "Sarah McGowan's goal: Be out of student debt by the time she turns 25. By maintaining a frugal lifestyle right out of college and working every chance she got, McGowan got rid of a little over $36,000 in debt in just under two years.

DeShena Woodard, a nurse from Texas, had nothing in savings and lived paycheck to paycheck until she changed her habits and paid off more than $50,000 in almost three years.

When Steven Donovan didn't want to plug his debt numbers into a budget app, he knew he had to act. Attacking his most-hated debt helped him pay off $118,000 in five years.

Sonia Sears ended up deep in the red while pursuing her "best life" in college and beyond. But she conquered her mountain of debt by working more, traveling less and moving back home. She paid off $79,000 in just over two years.

Ben and Melissa Panter were always frugal, but when they faced a large mortgage and growing student loan balances, they knew they had to kick frugality into high gear. The Panters paid off $127,000 in nearly four years.

Christmas gifts piled on top of existing debt persuaded Anthony Hartzog and his wife to act and pay off $114,151 in 23 months."

I know I included a lot of these stories, but every time I went to edit them down to one or two I just couldn't because I love seeing all of these different circumstances for getting out of debt. I really wanted you to see it doesn't matter how much debt you have, you can do it!

These stories each have different amounts and timelines but the one thing they have in common is they were all able to get out of debt. I know that you can too!

WHAT SHOULD I DO TO GET OUT OF DEBT?

You have to create a *Debt Payoff Plan,* which is exactly what it sounds like, a plan to get rid of your debt. Paying off debt is both a financial and a mental commitment. On the financial side you have to find the cash to pay off your debt and on the mental side you have to mentally commit and find a strategy that works for you. There is no one size fits all perfect way of getting out of debt but there are a few key components in all successful *Debt Payoff Plans* that you will need in order to permanently rid yourself of debt.

You must:

1. Decide to tackle your debt and make it a priority
2. Permanently change the behaviors that got you into debt
3. Find ways to increase your cash flow to repay the debt

I know you might be scared looking at how much debt you have but I promise that ignoring the problem will not make it go away and oftentimes will make it worse.

The first step truly is admitting that there is a problem and committing to do something about it. No more living in denial telling yourself, "It's not that bad." It might not be that bad, but it's certainly not good, and you are not doing yourself any favors.

Second, you have to change the behaviors that got you into debt in the first place. It's no good if you get rid of your existing debt just to find yourself a few months later piling on even more loans and right back in debt again. Even winning the lottery won't solve your financial problems if you don't learn how to spend less than you earn and live within your means.

It doesn't really matter what got you into debt in the first place, there are lots of reasons why people take out loans, some of them very valid reasons, others less so. Education, job loss, medical emergencies, compulsive shopping addictions, car trouble, or sometimes just overspending. What matters is that you learn from your mistakes and don't let it happen again. That you learn to only take out a loan when you have a solid *Debt Payoff Plan* in place with the income and ability to repay it in a timely fashion.

Here are a few examples of how to learn from your past mistakes:

1. If you borrowed $40,000 to buy a car but the car loan payments were so high you were stretched every month, then do NOT upgrade to an even more expensive car a year later with

even more expensive loan payments. Instead buy a less expensive car or save up money to buy your next car with cash.

2. If you maxed out your credit card on a shopping spree at Nordstroms, then do NOT spend money on any more clothes until you have paid off all the debt on your credit card for your current clothes.
3. If you lost your job and didn't have an emergency fund set up so you had to borrow money to pay your bills, then do NOT leave debt as your only option when emergencies happen. Work to save up an emergency fund so this will NOT happen again.
4. If you know you overspend every month on DoorDash purchases then delete the app from your phone and do NOT even have it as an option to tempt you. (Guilty)

I know behavior change is hard, especially if you've been living it up and have grown used to a certain lifestyle. But the hard truth is, if you can't afford it right now you must find a way to change. Now, it's not all bad, this isn't what it has to be like forever, just temporarily until you get everything back in order. This leads us to the third key component to a successful *Debt Payoff Plan.*

Third, you have to find ways to increase your cash flow to repay your debt. As we learned Income - Expenses = Cash Flow and so to increase your cash flow you must increase your income, decrease your expenses, or both. To put it simply, you must pay attention to your money and apply good money management habits.

Although spending less and lowering your expenses will help, it can only take you so far. In order to live within your means your cash flow will always be limited by the income number at the top. To really speed up your *Debt Payoff Plan,* you simply need to find ways to earn more money.

Whether that is finding a second part time job as an Uber driver, switching to a higher paying job, asking for a promotion, selling stuff on Craigslist, or starting a YouTube channel. There are lots of ways to create additional income but it is up to you to find them. Not everyone has to earn more money to get out of debt, but it sure does speed up the process.

Okay so remember the three key components to successfully rid yourself of debt are to:

1. Decide to tackle your debt
2. Change your behaviors
3. Increase your cash flow

Now, let's look at some of the best strategies to attack your debt!

WHICH DEBT DO I START WITH?

I would suggest prioritizing your debt using one of these two methods, either:

1. **Avalanche method** - get rid of debt with the highest interest rate first
2. **Snowball method** - get rid of debt with the lowest balance first

Avalanche Method - If you want to save more of your money and are okay with a little bit of delayed gratification then the debt avalanche method may be right for you. With this method your focus is on paying off the debt with the highest interest rate first (while still covering at least the minimum balances on your other debt). By focusing on the highest interest debt you eliminate the most expensive debt first and speed up your process to become debt-free.

Typically credit card debt has the highest interest rates. The interest rate is basically how much that company is charging you to borrow their money. If I owe two people $100 each and one person is charging me 25% interest and the other person is charging me 3% interest, then I am going to pay off the person with the higher 25% interest rate first because the money I borrowed from them is more expensive.

Here is an example of a *Debt Payoff Plan* using the

avalanche method by putting an extra $200 towards the debt with the highest interest rate first.

Debt Payoff Plan – Avalanche

Pay $200 in extra principal towards the loan with highest interest rate

Lender & Type	Loan Balance	Interest	Maturity	Payment
Amex: CC	$4,500	25.5%	10/01/21	$175 + $200
Chase: CC	$6,500	18.4%	05/31/22	$220
Toyota: Car	$20,500	9.5%	09/30/27	$540
Fannie Mae: College	$9,000	4.3%	05/30/25	$245
Wells Fargo: Mtg	$380,000	4.2%	08/22/48	$1,850
Mom & Dad: Personal	$2,500	0%	TBD	$100
TOTAL	$423,000			$3,330

Of the two approaches the avalanche method is my favorite but there are some cases where the snowball method works best.

Snowball Method - If small quick wins early on in the process help you stay motivated, then the debt snowball method may be right for you. With this approach, you put all the extra money you can towards paying your smallest debt first. Once you have the first debt paid off, you roll that money into paying the next smallest debt until all your debt is paid off. You are building momentum like a snowball rolling down the mountain. It starts small and it gets bigger and bigger.

Here is an example of a *Debt Payoff Plan* using the snowball method by putting an extra $200 towards the debt with the lowest balance first.

Debt Payoff Plan – Snowball

Pay $200 in extra principal towards the loan with lowest loan balance

Lender & Type	Loan Balance	Interest	Maturity	Payment
Mom & Dad: Personal	$2,500	0%	TBD	$100 + $200
Amex: CC	$4,500	25.5%	10/01/21	$175
Chase: CC	$6,500	18.4%	05/31/22	$220
Fannie Mae: College	$9,000	4.3%	05/30/25	$245
Toyota: Car	$20,500	9.5%	09/30/27	$540
Wells Fargo: Mtg	$380,000	4.2%	08/22/48	$1,850
TOTAL	$423,000			$3,330

When it comes to choosing a strategy the decision is personal, so the best thing for you to do is to develop a plan that you are motivated by even if it looks a little different from someone else's. As long as you've found a way that works, you're all set!

Remember you want to pay down the principal on these debts. You will still have to pay your minimum monthly payment on each debt, which includes interest and principal but when we are paying the debt down with additional payments we want to start lowering the actual outstanding loan balance by putting extra money towards principal.

WHAT IS DEBT CONSOLIDATION?

You may want to consider debt consolidation in order to make your debt easier to manage and less expensive overall. Two solid options for debt consolidation are:

1. A personal loan
2. A balance transfer to a credit card with 0% interest

If you have a lot of loans that all have different interest rates and payment due dates, sometimes that can be a chore to manage separately. If you are able to roll your debt into one loan with a lower interest rate it will help simplify what you have to keep track of and you will not have to spend as much with a lower interest rate. You can find unsecured personal loans to consolidate multiple loans into one monthly affordable payment. Plus, if you've been working to improve your credit score you may even get a lower interest rate with a personal loan.

The good thing about the personal loan is that your debt is restructured with a fixed loan term, usually 3 to 5 years and a fixed monthly payment. It is not revolving, it is a term loan, so you will not be tempted to draw the line up or borrow additional money, you know exactly what your payment is, and you can pay off your debt by the end of the loan term.

Another option is a balance transfer to a credit card with 0% interest. Keep in mind the 0% interest rate offer on balance transfers usually lasts for between 18 - 20 months, so this is only giving you a little bit of extra time. Make sure you pay off the debt before the 18 months are up and before the 0% interest rate jumps up to a much higher interest rate, otherwise, you could find yourself back where you started with high interest rate debt. Also, once you transfer your original debt to the 0% interest card, do NOT add any new debt to the old credit cards. Put those credit cards in time out, they have been overworked and need a long break. Cut them up, stick them in the freezer, hide them in a drawer, throw them away. Do whatever you need to do to ensure you won't use them.

Finally, there are two last resort strategies to consider with your debt and these are:

1. Debt settlement
2. Bankruptcy

Debt settlement is a negotiation with your lender or collections agency in which your lender agrees to accept a partial payment to satisfy your debt rather than the full loan balance. This strategy will work best for people who can afford to make a large one time settlement payment to their lender. Lenders may be open to a debt settlement if you'vc had special extenuating circumstances, such as a job loss, medical emergency, or divorce.

Lastly, if your debts are so out of control that they

have grown insurmountable, bankruptcy may be a path to consider. This should be your last resort because bankruptcy will destroy your creditworthiness. Do not make this decision lightly, bankruptcy is usually a long and expensive process that involves attorneys and court filing fees. Before filing bankruptcy you must also seek credit counseling approved by the Department of Justice. This is definitely a last resort option and my advice is you should do everything you can to avoid it.

If you do proceed, you can file for 2 types of personal bankruptcy which are:

1. Chapter 7: which requires you to surrender some of your property
2. Chapter 13: which allows you to keep your property.

I know sometimes when you are being harassed by collection agencies and surrounded by past due bills, it feels as if there is no way out. But by using some of the strategies above you can eventually free yourself from the shackles of debt.

There are also lots of debt payoff apps that can help you get rid of your debt. All you really need is a smartphone to try out some of these debt payoff apps and finally make some progress. They each have their pros and cons, but ultimately, the best debt payoff app is the one you consistently use!

Also, although I think it goes without saying, I'm going

to say it anyway. While you are paying down your debt, do not go and obtain more debt! That will take you 2 steps backward. No more loans until you've tackled the ones you already have.

That reminds me, there are these things called internet lenders or payday loans that you need to look out for. Sometimes we need a little bit of cash on short notice, and these lenders can provide that. Not all of them are bad and there is a reason they exist. However, it is so important that you read the fine script before obtaining a loan with an internet lender.

For example, have you seen the Netflix series *Dirty Money*? One of the episodes shows a lender which gave out predatory loans that had very unclear repayment terms in the contract. When the clients started getting calls from the company to make payments on their loan they thought that they were paying back the principal on their loan (the amount they borrowed) but in fact those were just interest payments. Months went by with clients making these large interest payments until they found out that their whole loan balance was still due and that none of those payments went towards their outstanding loan balance.

My point is just that you need to know what you are paying and to whom. Whether you are paying both principal and interest, or just interest with your payments, and if your money is going where you intended for it to go. Cash advance loans or payday loans are a very slippery slope, which I do not recommend, and if you do obtain one proceed with extreme caution and pay it off ASAP.

IS THERE SUCH A THING AS GOOD DEBT?

Believe it or not, debt can sometimes be a good thing. There is a time and place when you should use debt to your advantage, and this good debt is often referred to as leverage because you are leveraging someone else's money.

It can be a good thing to use leverage for investments or for appreciating assets that will produce more income. However, it is a bad thing to obtain debt when it is used for consumption. When debt is used for consumption it will actually do more harm than good to your financial picture. It is wise to only obtain good debt and pay off your bad debt or not get into it in the first place.

- Bad debt = used for consumption
- Good debt = used for investments

A simple way to think about good debt vs. bad debt is that bad debt takes money out of your pocket and good debt has the potential to put money into your pocket.

For example, a line of credit with a credit card is a bad debt because people most often use it to buy depreciating items such as TVs, phones, cars, and clothes or for consumption such as for alcohol, food, and entertainment. There is no real potential for future income or capital gains from any of these things. That money is gone as soon as you make your purchase and will not come back to produce any form of income.

Conversely, a loan for an investment property can be good debt because you are buying an appreciating asset, a house. You can either rent out that house for more than the mortgage payment for positive cash flow, which would put more money into your pocket, or sell the house in the future for capital gains, which would put more money into your pocket. It has the potential to put money back into your pocket, so I would consider obtaining debt to help purchase it. Education is another investment you could consider as good debt because, in general, the more education a person has, the greater their earning potential.

Of course, it is possible to invest in education or a real estate property that does not produce more income or money, so you have to be very intentional with your investments and consider the return on investment (ROI) you expect to receive with each investment you make. I only consider obtaining debt for education, real estate, or other appreciating assets when there is a very clear ROI that would put money back into my pocket.

MONEY MOVERS

- Create your *Debt Payoff Plan*. Decide on either the avalanche or snowball method and which loan to start with. Determine the amount you will pay towards the principal of your loan.

- Set up an automatic payment to your loan account every month.
- Sign up for a debt payoff app.
- Consolidate your loans if necessary.

SIMPLER, QUICKER, AND EASIER

"Wealth is the ability to fully experience life." - Henry David Thoreau

Congratulations, you are doing great! You have identified your financial values and goals, have a *Saving & Spending Plan,* as well as a *Debt Payoff Plan*! You are amazing! The hard part is over, take a deep breath!

Getting to this point alone will double your likelihood of success with your finances. You are aware of what your finances look like and have a plan to start improving your financial picture!

This is a truly great place to be and I am so proud of you. What do you say to us making it even simpler, easier, and quicker to manage your finances?

Yes? Okay great, now we are going to make it even easier to monitor your finances and accomplish your goals.

I've always found that to really set ourselves up for success when improving our finances for the first time we need to change our ENVIRONMENT and our BEHAVIORS. We all have ingrained habits and surroundings that have led to where we are currently. When we make a big change we need to take a look at those surroundings and habits and ensure they will help us succeed and not trip us up.

For example, when I am trying to lose weight I know I need to burn more calories (with exercise) and eat less calories (with a meal plan). When my body burns off more calories than I consume in a day I will lose weight. However, I also know that there is Smartfood white cheddar popcorn (so delicious!) in my pantry. By the end of the work day I am tired with barely any self-discipline left and will be tempted to reach for the white cheddar popcorn and eat the whole delicious bag in one sitting while watching Netflix.

In order to set myself up for success I have to change my environment. If I do not have white cheddar popcorn in the house because I did not buy it at the grocery store, then I don't have to worry about fighting with my self-discipline at the end of the day. It simply isn't an option so I won't reach for it. If I buy apples and make sure to have them in the house then an apple is an option, so I will grab an apple and my environment has set me up for success with a healthy lower calorie option for a snack.

We want to do the same thing with our finances by structuring our financial environment for success. We want to give ourselves the best possible environment and habits to help us succeed and there are quite a few easy ways to do that.

WHAT IS THE IDEAL FINANCIAL SET UP TO MAKE THIS SIMPLER?

We are going to start by financially cleaning house. The same way we organize our homes, declutter our bedrooms, and clean up our kitchens we need to organize our finances, declutter our extra accounts, and clean up our outstanding loan balances. Here is what you need to do.

I'd like you to clean up your finances so you only have:

- One checking account
- One investment account provider
- One individual retirement account (IRA)
- One company sponsored retirement account (401K)
- One credit card for your personal expenses

Let's play a little game? Do you notice the word that is the same in each of these bullets?

Yup, ONE. To keep your finances as simple as possible, I recommend having only one of each of these accounts to start.

Now I know some of you might say, "What about diversification with different account providers in case something were to happen to the company that owns my account? It might be better to have my money and investments all spread out in different companies."

True, there is something to be said for spreading out the company risk, however, I'm talking about what makes your finances the easiest to keep track of to start out. To create strong healthy financial habits that you will stick to, you are best served by keeping it simple.

Once you are looking at your financial statements every single month and have been for over a year then we can move into more advanced investment strategies and diversify your accounts. Until then let's just keep it simple and straightforward and start with one of each account.

Now I know you might be wondering, "But what if I already have a bunch of different accounts?"

That's okay. Your goal at the end of this chapter is to consolidate your finances so you have just one of each of these accounts.

Checking Account - Only one checking account for your personal finances, so that you have just one spot that your income and expenses flow in and out of. This way you can always see exactly what your cash flow looks like at any point in time with all income and expenses connected to the same account.[1]

Investment Account - Only one investment account provider for your different financial goals. Stick to just one investment account provider to start. With that one provider you can create different investment accounts for each of your financial goals. That way when you are tracking your finances you have just one place to log in to review your investments, but you can still easily track each of your goals.

For example, if you use E*Trade as your investment provider you can set up one account for your emergency fund, another account to save for a downpayment on a house, and a third account for that vacation to the Bahamas.

Individual Retirement Account - One individual retirement account (IRA) where you consolidate all of your 401Ks or previous retirement accounts from past jobs. I know what it's like moving from job to job and having these lingering retirement accounts for your previous jobs out there. It gets confusing trying to track them all down and remember what the website and login is for each and every one. Do yourself a favor and whenever you switch jobs, roll all of your old 401Ks or retirement accounts into one IRA. It will make it so much easier to keep track of, and since I'm guessing you are probably like me and did not do this every time you switched jobs, go ahead and tackle this right now. I know it is a pain, but just get it over with, find all those old retirement plans and move them all into one rollover IRA.

Company Sponsored Retirement Account - One company sponsored retirement account, such as a 401K, where your current job will match your contributions. You still want to take advantage of the benefits of company matches from your current job so go ahead and have one company sponsored retirement account with your current job. Just remember, if you change companies to roll that old retirement account into your rollover IRA.

Remember to contribute AT LEAST enough to get your company's match amount. If your company will match up to a 4% contribution in your retirement account then at least contribute 4%. This is free money being provided by your company. By all means take advantage of it!

Credit Card - One and ONLY one personal credit card for your personal expenses. This is the one I see most often abused that leads to financial distress. Remember how we are trying to set up your environment for success. Minimizing your credit cards has a HUGE impact on this.

Every single credit card you have is a loan, they are revolving lines of credit, and you are borrowing money.

credit card = revolving line of credit = a loan = debt

Since every single credit card is another loan, the less loans you have to keep track of the better. Let's narrow it all the way down to just one.

I know it can be very tempting to sign up for all these different credit cards with so many different benefits and points but do NOT do it. We want to simplify things and when you have all these different credit cards that you have to track down every month, it can create such a hassle when you are trying to figure out what you've already spent on expenses for that month.

Pick your favorite credit card and charge all of your

purchases to this one card every month. Then pay the balance off COMPLETELY at the end of the month. For all of your other credit cards that you didn't pick, pay them off until they have a $0 balance.

Random but important aside - notice I did not say cancel your other credit cards, I just said to pay them off. I want to be clear that you do not want to cancel your current credit cards, as it will have a negative impact on your credit score, but I do want you to stop using them and pay them off. I am suggesting you just take your extra credit cards and put them in your sock drawer or cut them up so you aren't tempted to use them and pay all the credit card balances down to $0. You can keep your favorite credit card and only use that one going forward.

When you have just one credit card it is so much easier to track. Use the one card for all your purchases, pay it off every month, build up your credit history, and then start taking advantage of some of the card benefits. We want your credit score to go up and this will help to do that!

This is how you start to game the system and take full advantage of your credit card points for some really awesome and fun perks in the process. My fiancé is amazing at this and we have literally been able to take all-inclusive trips to gorgeous Caribbean beach locations with our flights and resorts completely covered by credit card points. So, just trust me on this. One credit card.

Other Accounts - I know there will be other accounts you have as well such as your mortgage loan account. My goal here is for you to simplify so you have as few accounts to keep track of as possible. We only want one provider whenever possible so that we can easily keep track of all of your accounts in your financial app, without having to log in to 100 different places to get an idea of what your financial picture looks like.

The same principle applies if you have student loans, consolidate them all into one provider to make it as simple as possible to keep track of.

It may take you a little bit of time to consolidate these accounts, but it will save you time when you prepare your monthly financial statements and will really simplify your finances so they are easy to review each and every month.

Okay so go ahead, put your financial gloves on and clean house, you will feel so much better once you do!

HOW CAN WE MAKE THIS EVEN QUICKER?

I have a friend who we will call Alice and she was deeply in debt. She did not have a *Debt Payoff Plan,* but she did set up her bank account to automatically deposit her car payment on the 5th of each month, so she never had to look at it or deal with it. Out of site, out of mind!

Alice would receive weekly calls from a collection agency, which she would ignore. After a few years she'd had enough of all the collection calls, was ready to get out of debt, and was determined to get her finances in order. She started to create a budget, and was looking for ways to build up an emergency fund. She made up her mind that the next time a random 1-800 number called her cell phone, instead of silencing it, she would answer and deal with whatever it was that was facing her on the other end of the line. She was determined to dig herself out of debt!

Eventually the dreaded 1-800 number called her cell phone and she pumped herself up to answer it. The voice on the other end asked if it was Alice they were speaking to and stated that they have been trying to get in touch with her for some time. Alice replied that it was indeed her and she was sorry for ignoring the calls, but was ready to speak to them.

To Alice's surprise, they weren't calling to try and collect a debt. In fact, it was quite the opposite. They were responsible for handling Alice's auto loan and they were desperately trying to get in touch with her to tell her to stop sending them money. Alice had been making automatic monthly payments to them for years without giving it a second thought. Not only had Alice already paid off the car loan balance in full, but she had been sending them extra payments for months. Imagine that!

They had collected all of her extra payments and needed to give that money back to her. Needless to say, Alice was in complete shock. She found out she didn't owe them any more, they had money to give her, and she now had just what she needed to build up her emergency fund!

Obviously, not everyone will be as lucky, (is lucky the right word?) as Alice, but it does go to show that when you face your finances, it's not always as bad as you imagine it will be. Plus, there really is incredible power with automatic payments, automatic saving, and automatic investing and you can use this power to your advantage.

Automation is your friend and makes paying your bills and saving and investing SO much quicker and easier. Do everything you can to use automation to your advantage.

Financial success is not hard when you create the right systems and processes to succeed. The key is to create a system that limits bad behaviors and encourages good behaviors that help future you. This is taking our self-discipline out of the picture, so you don't have to try and find the willpower every day, every week, and every month to make the right choices. Instead structure your finances to make the right choices for you.

I mean really how nice would it be if your bills were all paid on time every month, without you even thinking about it? What if you could spend guilt-free knowing you were automatically saving towards your goals? What if you were investing in all the right places without lifting a finger?

For example, setting up an automatic deposit into your investment account for your emergency fund every month. This requires only a little bit of effort up front and then virtually no effort thereafter and you have the comfort of knowing you are covering yourself for any unexpected rainy days.

There are 5 ways to automate your finances:

1. Automate your paycheck

2. Automate your company sponsored retirement savings
3. Automate your investing
4. Automate your bills and loan payments
5. Review and increase your automated transfers and payments

First, automate your paycheck to direct deposit into your primary checking account every month. Most companies have the ability to do this and it is the easiest and most convenient way to be paid.

Second, automate your paycheck to direct deposit into your company sponsored retirement plan, such as a 401K every month. At a minimum you should automatically invest at least the % that your employer will match. If your employer will match up to 3% of your contributions then put at least 3% of your paycheck into the company sponsored retirement plan. That is just free money on the table and I highly encourage you to take full advantage of it.

Third, set up automated recurring transfers to your investment accounts. If you haven't set up your investment accounts yet, now is the time to open up these accounts. Remember you want to have an investment account for your emergency fund and other financial goals as well as an individual retirement account (IRA) to rollover all of your old retirement accounts.

Remember, as I mentioned before, ensure you build up a little bit of a buffer in your checking account to prevent any overdraft fees before you initiate your recurring transfers. A buffer of about one month's worth of expenses will keep you covered. If on average you spend about $3,500 a month in expenses just keep an extra $3,500 buffer in your checking account at all times.

Fourth, set up automatic payments for your bills and loan payments. Almost all of your utility bills, mortgage loans, auto loans, credit card loans, student loans, and insurance can be set up to be paid automatically. Look up when each of these bills is due, change the due dates to the end of the month if you can, and then set up your automatic payment to occur 1-2 days before the bill or loan payment is due. Remember, for the credit card we want to pay the entire balance off at the end of each month, not just the minimum payment.

Fifth, the last step in the process is to consistently review your automated payments and transfers and adjust as needed. Ideally, we want to increase our automated investments over time. When you review your financial statements each month, see if you can begin to increase the amount you are automatically investing.

Sometimes you can even set up an automatic escalation. For example, if you know you usually have a pay raise every year, you can set up an automatic escalation to increase the amount or percent you invest into your retirement account right after you receive your annual pay raise.

Okay, that's it! Those are the 5 things to know for automating your finances.

The beauty of automation is once you have all your savings, investments, bills and loan payments automated and paid each month, anything left over in your account at the end of the month is fun money! You don't have to be like, "Oh I better go transfer that to savings or put it towards my loan," because you've already been there, done that, and it is taken care of.

Now you can have a little fun and take any leftover cash flow for the month and put it towards whatever you want! You can spend any leftover money guilt-free knowing you are already paying off your loans and are saving towards your goals. Go enjoy a nice dinner with your family! Have a fun shopping spree at Target! Treat yourself!

I do know that this system will take a little bit of time to set up and be a little bit of effort on the front end, but trust me IT WILL BE WORTH IT. Once it is all set up, you are automatically on the right path to accomplish your financial goals. You don't have to rely on your self-discipline and willpower every month, your system will all just seamlessly work for you. It is wonderful because you are not only creating additional money for your future self but also additional time for yourself. If you put in a little bit of work and time up front, then you will get extra time and money (from saved interest and investments) back to you every single month.

WHAT NEW HABITS WILL MAKE THIS EASIER?

The more we do something the easier it becomes. In order to do something more consistently, we have to engrain it as a good habit. When we set a new healthy habit, we can put ourselves on autopilot and on the path to success.

So, let's take a look at some good habits to make monitoring our personal finances as easy and second nature as possible.

The first is for calendar reminders to prepare your financial statements every month. You really want to turn this into a habit as soon as possible. Repetition is key. I don't want you to prepare your financial statements just this once and then forget how to do it and never prepare them again. I want you to be able to pull all this information together so quickly and easily that it becomes second nature.

We already know we need to prepare our financial statements once a month at least, but when?

I like to prepare them all on the 1st day of the month. For example, on October 1st, I will sit down and prepare my financial statements for month end September as of September 30th. In regards to the best time of day, for me the best time to do this is in the morning. That way I make sure to get it done before all my other tasks build up. I pay off the full outstanding balance of my credit cards, pay any other month end bills, and prepare my month end financial statements. When I use my financial apps to help me prepare these financial statements I can usually prepare all of them in under 30 minutes.

Since this will still be new for you, the first few times you go through and do this it will probably take a little longer just because you are learning. But once you get the hang of it I know that it won't take you very long at all and you'll be amazed at how easy it can really be.

So, go ahead and put a recurring calendar reminder on your schedule right now for the 1st of every month for at least 30 minutes. Pick a time that you know will work for your schedule and prioritize it. Set your intention right now to make your finances a priority every month and there is no doubt in my mind that they will begin improving.

I've found it is very helpful when you are establishing new habits to layer the new habits into your old or existing habits. Is there something you can attach this new habit onto so you won't forget?

For example, right after I finish breakfast I will prepare my monthly financial statements or before going to the grocery store I check my total expenses number on my financial app to see how I'm doing with my spending for the month. I stack a new habit onto something I am already routinely doing to make sure that it gets done.

Is there something that you do every day, that you could easily layer checking your financial apps and preparing your financial statements into?

Please just find a way to use the financial apps! Get into the habit of checking them consistently. Make them front and center on your phone home screen so they are the first thing you see when you look at your phone.

To implement your *Saving & Spending Plan* you have to have an idea of what your spending looks like throughout the month and the absolute easiest and best way I've seen to do that is with one of the apps we talked about. That way when it comes time to prepare your *Income & Expense Statement* you will be happy to see you have positive cash flow for the month instead of disappointed that you aren't meeting your goals.

A recent study showed that the average person that downloads and uses a budgeting app three times per week, reduced their discretionary spending by almost 12%.

If you are really committed to improving your finances, my suggestion is you check your app every week. Yup, I said it, EVERY WEEK. It is a good check to see at the end of each week how much you have spent. Then if you spent more than you thought that week, you still have some time to adjust your spending before the end of the month instead of getting to the end of the month and finding out you blew way past your spending goal and it is too late to do anything about it.

Plus, it helps you get all the kinks worked out up front. Every time you check your app you will get more and more used to it and faster at knowing what to look for.

Then just make sure you have your recurring reminder with a little bit of time blocked off for the 1st of every month to prepare your financial statements. That way when the next month rolls around and it's time for you to prepare them you will still remember how and know exactly what to do. At first it might take you longer but once you get the hang of this I promise it doesn't take much time at all. I usually have mine completed in under 30 minutes.

Let's go ahead and start making this simpler, quicker, and easier right now with our money movers.

MONEY MOVERS

- Clean house and simplify your financial accounts to ONE of each account type.
- Automate your paycheck, retirement saving, investing, bills, and loan payments every month.
- Set a monthly reminder to prepare and review your financial statements and financial plans every month.
- Check your financial apps and spending weekly to stay on track.

THE END…ALMOST!

Book reviews are not easy to come by.

As an independent author with a tiny marketing budget, I rely on readers, like you, to leave a short review on Amazon.

Even if it is just a sentence of two!

So, if you enjoyed the book, please go to Amazon and leave a review.

Thank you from the bottom of my heart for purchasing this book and reading it to the end! It means the world to me and I wish you the very best in your financial endeavors!

CONCLUSION

You did it!!!! I am so INCREDIBLY PROUD of you for finishing this book! You have officially faced your finances and I know you will be a better person for it! Not to mention how much better your finances are going to become over these upcoming months and years.

I encourage you to re-read any chapters you need to and use this book as a reference guide as much as possible. There is a lot in here so go back through it as many times as you need to and make sure you tackle all those money movers at the end of each chapter. Again, I am so so proud of you for making it this far.

In the first half of the book you've learned how to understand your current financial condition. You can now prepare and review the 3 most important financial statements for your personal finances:

- *Income & Expense Statement*

- *Net Worth Statement*
- *Debt Schedule*

You've looked at all your dreaded bank accounts and, you know what, you survived!

In the second half of the book you've learned how to plan for your financial future. You've identified what you value and what you really want to accomplish with your money and your financial goals. You know why it is important to take action now to improve your financial future. You are crafting the life you truly want and it's time for you to feel the joy of achieving your financial dreams.

You've created real actionable plans to improve your finances going forward with your:

- *Saving & Spending Plan*
- *Debt Payoff Plan*

You know how to set up your emergency fund to take care of yourself and your family for any of those unexpected surprises. You've seen the debt you have and it's okay because now you have a plan to start getting rid of it. You're finally in control of your money, instead of letting it control you. You even know how you can start investing your money easily with robo advisors right away.

And you've learned how to make your finances even simpler by organizing your financial accounts. You know how to make it quicker with an automated system in place. You know how to make it even easier with the right habits and financial apps at your fingertips.

If there is just one thing that I want you to take away from this book, it is that YOU are in control of your finances and YOU are in control of your future. With a little time and effort I know that you can do anything you set your mind to! Thank you for facing your finances with me.

Go forth and prosper my wonderful CFOs, you've got this!

NOTES

INTRODUCTION

1. According to a study from the National Endowment for Financial Education.

4. NET WORTH STATEMENT

1. In the business world, this is called the *Balance Sheet* instead of the *Net Worth Statement.* When you take the business' assets and subtract the business' liabilities you are left with the company's shareholder's equity.
   Assets - Liabilities = Shareholder's Equity
2. Only include the cash surrender value of a life insurance policy; do not include the death benefit amount. The cash surrender value is the amount of money the insurance company would return to you if you terminated the policy.
3. To calculate your business equity take the business' Assets - Liabilities = Equity and multiply by % ownership. For example: Let's say the business has $200K in Assets, $150K in Liabilities and I have 60% ownership and my sister has 40% ownership. $200K - $150K = $50K * 60% = $30K in business equity.
4. Kelly Blue Book is usually a good place to estimate the current value of your car.

8. SIMPLER, QUICKER, AND EASIER

1. The only exception is if you also own and operate a small business. If that is the case then you should have separate checking accounts for your personal finances and your business finances.

REFERENCES

Aaron. "9 Questions That Will Help You Discover Your Financial Values." *Personal Finance For Beginners,* 2021, https://www.personalfinanceforbeginners.com/financial-values-questions/. Accessed 24 August 2021.

Amanda. "Using Your Values to Make the Best Money Decisions." *Women Who Money,* 11 November 2019, https://womenwhomoney.com/values-money-decisions/. Accessed 24 August 2021.

Andrew. "How to Create Your Personal Net Worth Statement (And Why You Need It)." *WealthyNickel,* 21 May 2019, https://wealthynickel.com/personal-net-worth-statement/. Accessed 03 August 2021.

Bieber, Christy. "How to Figure Out Your Total Debt Balance." *The Ascent,* 21 July 2019, https://www.fool.com/the-ascent/banks/articles/how-figure-out-your-total-debt-balance/. Accessed 05 August 2021.

Bond, Casey. "6 Debt Payoff Apps You'll Want To

Download ASAP." *Huffpost,* 07 December 2018, https://www.huffpost.com/entry/debt-apps-iphone-android_n_5c0985a2e4b0b6cdaf5d3e29. Accessed 06 August 2021.

Bose, Shubhomita. "89% of Millennial Women Online Shoppers Are Waiting for Your Next Sale, Survey Finds." *Small Business Trends,* 08 November 2017, https://smallbiztrends.com/2017/11/shopping-habits-of-millennial-women.html. Accessed 01 September 2021.

The Brain. "The Framework: Your Life as a Profit and Loss Statement and Balance Sheet." *The Finance Brain,* 20 July 2018, https://thefinancebrain.com/2018/07/20/the-framework-your-life-as-a-profit-and-loss-statement-and-balance-sheet/. Accessed 03 August 2021.

Carter, Timothy. "The True Failure Rate of Small Businesses." *Entrepreneur,* 03 January 2021, https://www.entrepreneur.com/article/361350. Accessed 10 August 2021.

Charles Schwab. "Roth IRA vs. Traditional IRA." *Charles Schwab,* 2021, https://www.schwab.com/ira/understand-iras/roth-vs-trad-ira. Accessed 19 October 2021.

Davis, Krystle M. "20 Facts And Figures To Know When Marketing To Women." *Forbes,* 13 May 2019, https://www.forbes.com/sites/forbescontentmarketing/2019/05/13/20-facts-and-figures-to-know-when-marketing-to-women/?sh=7cc6557d1297. Accessed 01 September 2021.

DeMatteo, Megan, et al. "The beginner's guide to

credit scores: How to understand and improve your credit score." *CNBC,* 21 July 2021, https://www.cnbc.com/select/guide/credit-scores-for-beginners/. Accessed 05 August 2021.

Dore, Kate. "Best Budgeting Apps." *Investopedia,* 03 July 2021, https://www.investopedia.com/best-budgeting-apps-5085405#best-for-couples-zeta. Accessed 02 September 2021.

Egan, John. "How Do I Find Out What Debts I Owe?" *Experian,* 24 April 2021, https://www.experian.com/blogs/ask-experian/how-do-i-find-who-i-owe-money-to/. Accessed 05 August 2021.

El Issa, Erin. "2020 American Household Credit Card Debt Study." *NerdWallet,* 12 January 2021, https://www.nerdwallet.com/blog/average-credit-card-debt-household/#footnote-two. Accessed 06 August 2021.

Fawcett, Cory. "Why many doctors live paycheck to paycheck." *KevinMD.com,* 18 March 2019, https://www.kevinmd.com/blog/2019/03/why-many-doctors-live-paycheck-to-paycheck.html. Accessed 26 October 2021.

Folger, Jean. "Why Knowing Your Net Worth Is Important." *Investopedia,* 23 June 2021, https://www.investopedia.com/articles/pf/13/importance-of-knowing-your-net-worth.asp. Accessed 03 August 2021.

Fontinelle, Amy. "Top Sources for Free Credit Scores." *Investopedia,* 06 May 2021, https://www.investopedia.com/articles/personal-finance/091714/top-websites-checking-your-credit-scores.asp. Accessed 05 August 2021.

Harkness, Brendan. "How to Pay Off Debt: 6 Strategies That Work." *Credit Card Insider*, 08 January 2021, https://www.creditcardinsider.com/learn/reducing-debt/. Accessed 06 August 2021.

Hynes, Casey. "Pay off Your Debts With These 10 Mobile Debt Apps." *Student Loan Hero*, 20 March 2020, https://studentloanhero.com/featured/awesome-debt-payoff-mobile-apps/. Accessed 06 August 2021.

Irby, Latoya. "Best Free Credit Reports." *The Balance*, 07 April 2021, https://www.thebalance.com/best-free-credit-reports-4174784. Accessed 05 August 2021.

James, Geoffrey. "What Goal-Setting Does to Your Brain and Why It's Spectacularly Effective." *Inc.com*, 23 October 2019, https://www.inc.com/geoffrey-james/what-goal-setting-does-to-your-brain-why-its-spectacularly-effective.html. Accessed 24 August 2021.

Jayakumar, Amrita. "How They Ditched Debt." *Nerd-Wallet*, 2021, https://www.nerdwallet.com/article/finance/getting-out-of-debt-stories. Accessed 02 November 2021.

Johnson, Carrie. "Financial Values, Attitudes and Goals." *North Dakota State University*, January 2021, https://www.ag.ndsu.edu/publications/money/financial-values-attitudes-and-goals. Accessed 26 August 2021.

Kiyosaki, Robert. "New Rule of Money #2: Learn How to Use Good Debt vs. Bad Debt." *Rich Dad*, 17 March 2020, https://www.richdad.com/good-debt-vs-bad-debt. Accessed 06 August 2021.

Lazaroff, Peter. "How To Automate Your Finances In 5

Easy Steps." *Forbes,* 17 January 2018, https://www.forbes.com/sites/peterlazaroff/2018/01/17/how-to-automate-your-finances-in-5-easy-steps/?sh=aaa1e99329a6. Accessed 02 September 2021.

Lorz, Kari. "Your Personal Core Values Are the Key to Setting & Reaching Your Goals." *Money for the Mamas,* 16 June 2019, https://www.moneyforthemamas.com/personal-core-values/. Accessed 25 August 2021.

Martin, Emmie. "Nicolas Cage once blew $150 million on a private island and a dinosaur skull—here's everything he bought." *CNBC.com,* 20 January 2018, https://www.cnbc.com/2018/01/19/how-nicholas-cage-once-blew-his-entire-150-million-fortune.html. Accessed 26 October 2021.

Martucci, Brian. "6 Rich Celebrities Who Went Broke and Declared Bankruptcy." *Money Crashers,* 12 December 2017, https://www.moneycrashers.com/bankrupt-celebrities-rich-broke/. Accessed 04 October 2021.

McClincy, Bob. "How Big is One Trillion Dollars?" *Exhibit City News,* 02 March 2021, https://exhibitcitynews.com/how-big-is-one-trillion-dollars/. Accessed 28 October 2021.

Miller, Walli. "Examples of Financial Goals." *Clever Girl Finance,* 31 July 2021, https://www.clevergirlfinance.com/blog/examples-of-financial-goals/. Accessed 24 August 2021.

Morin, Amy. "Starting A Business Without Debt: An Interview With Chris Hogan." *Forbes,* 03 March 2014, https://www.forbes.com/sites/amymorin/2014/03/03/

starting-a-business-without-debt-an-interview-with-chris-hogan/?sh=2e30cbef6f85. Accessed 10 August 2021.

Murray, Jean. "What Is a Personal Financial Statement?" *The Balance Small Business,* 30 June 2020, https://www.thebalancesmb.com/overview-of-personal-financial-statement-4148190. Accessed 03 August 2021.

NerdWallet. "The 7 Best Budget Apps for 2021." *NerdWallet,* 21 December 2020, https://www.nerdwallet.com/article/finance/best-budget-apps. Accessed 02 September 2021.

Oliver. "7 Different Types of Income Streams." *Penta,* February 2021, https://getpenta.com/en/blog/7-different-types-of-income-streams/. Accessed 26 August 2021.

O'Neill, Barbara. "Values, Goals and Financial Decisions." *Rutgers,* June 2016, https://njaes.rutgers.edu/money/pdfs/lesson-plans/DoE-Lesson-Plan-9-Values-Goals-and-Financial-Decisions.pdf. Accessed 24 August 2021.

Petrov, Christo. "20+ Incredible Personal Finance Statistics to Know in 2021." *SpendMeNot,* 06 August 2021, https://spendmenot.com/blog/personal-finance-statistics/. Accessed 28 August 2021.

Pyles, Sean. "How to Pay Off Debt Fast: 7 Tips." *NerdWallet,* 29 May 2020, https://www.nerdwallet.com/article/finance/find-extra-money-pay-debts. Accessed 06 August 2021.

Ramsey Solutions. "12 Reasons People Stay in Debt." *Ramsey,* 25 February 2021, https://www.ramseysolutions.

com/debt/why-do-people-stay-in-debt. Accessed 06 August 2021.

Roberts, Emily. "Values, Goals, and Tactics." *Personal Finance for PHDs,* 12 December 2014, http://pfforphds.com/values-goals-and-tactics/. Accessed 24 August 2021.

Rosenberg, Eric. "Best Budgeting Apps." *The Balance,* 02 July 2021, https://www.thebalance.com/best-budgeting-apps-4159414. Accessed 02 September 2021.

Sethi, Ramit. "The Ultimate Guide to Personal Finance." *I Will Teach You To Be Rich,* 2021, https://www.iwillteachyoutoberich.com/guides/ultimate-guide-to-personal-finance/#part2-automate-your-money. Accessed 02 September 2021.

Smart About My Money. "The Ultimate Guide to Creating Your Personal Financial Statement." *Smart About My Money,* http://www.smartaboutmymoney.com/the-ultimate-guide-to-creating-your-personal-financial-statement/. Accessed 03 August 2021.

Sokunbi, Bola. "How To Automate Your Finances." *Clever Girl Finance,* 24 April 2021, https://www.clevergirlfinance.com/blog/how-to-automate-finances/. Accessed 02 September 2021.

Vohwinkle, Jeremy. "How to Make a Personal Budget in 6 Easy Steps." *The Balance,* 15 May 2021, https://www.thebalance.com/how-to-make-a-budget-1289587. Accessed 27 August 2021.

Weliver, David. "How To Budget: 4 Easy Steps To Get You Started." *Money Under 30,* 27 June 2021, https://www.

moneyunder30.com/no-more-budgets. Accessed 28 August 2021.

Weliver, David. “Kick Debt's Butt! How To Get Out Of Debt On Your Own.” *Money Under 30,* 26 May 2021, https://www.moneyunder30.com/get-out-of-debt-on-your-own. Accessed 06 August 2021.

Yaged, Christine. “How Nicolas Cage Wildly Spent a $150 Million Fortune.” *FinanceBuzz.com,* 08 August 2021, https://financebuzz.com/finance-nicolas-cage-buying-spree. Accessed 26 October 2021.

Yih, Jim. “What are your family financial values?” *RetireHappy,* 16 January 2020, https://retirehappy.ca/your-family-financial-values/. Accessed 24 August 2021.

Printed in Great Britain
by Amazon

33143856R00128